Educational Courage

Educational Courage

Resisting the Ambush of Public Education

Nancy Schniedewind and
Mara Sapon-Shevin

Beacon Press, Boston

KH

Dedicated to the educational courage of all those
struggling for more democratic schools and to
Julia Grace Schniedewind and Rhoda Myra Ginsberg Sapon

BEACON PRESS
25 Beacon Street
Boston, Massachusetts 02108–2892
www.beacon.org

Beacon Press books
are published under the auspices of
the Unitarian Universalist Association of Congregations.

15   14   13   12   8   7   6   5   4   3   2   1

This book is printed on acid-free paper that meets the uncoated paper
ANSI/NISO specifications for permanence as revised in 1992.

Text design and composition by Wilsted & Taylor Publishing Services

A version of "A Nationwide Action to Save Our Schools" originally appeared on SocialistWorker
.org, August 2, 2011. "The Wisconsin Uprising," pieces by Bob Peterson, Stephanie Walters, and Kathy
Xiong, originally appeared in *Rethinking Schools* (Spring 2011). It is reprinted with permission. "De-
bunking the Case for National Standards," copyright © 2010 by Alfie Kohn, was originally published in
Education Week (January 2010). It is reprinted with the author's permission. "Arizona Students Protest
New Law Banning Ethnic Studies Classes" is reprinted with permission from Democracy Now! "Pensa-
miento Serpentine" appears in *Luís Valdez—Early Works*, copyright © Arte Público Press (University
of Houston). It is reprinted with permission. "The Curie 12" originally appeared in *City Kids, City
Teachers: Reports from the Front Row*, William Ayers and Patricia Ford, eds. (New Press, 2008). "The
Struggle against Mayoral Control in Milwaukee" was originally delivered as a speech at the Ninth
Trinational Conference for the Defense of Public Education, Montreal, May 8, 2010.

Library of Congress Cataloging-in-Publication Data
Educational courage : resisting the ambush of public education /
[edited by] Nancy Schniedewind and Mara Sapon-Shevin.
    p. cm.
Includes bibliographical references.
ISBN 978-0-8070-3295-4 (pbk.)
1. Public schools—United States. 2. Democracy and education—United States.
3. Educational change—United States. I. Schniedewind, Nancy.
II. Sapon-Shevin, Mara.
LA217.2.E385 2012
370.973—dc23   2012009323

Contents

Foreword

For thirty years, between 1968 and 1998, I was a part of a surprisingly vigorous educational reform movement that was slowly creeping its way into the mainstream. One part of me recognized that it was unlikely that the largely conservative political climate would be comfortable soil for seeding the kind of liberatory education I envisioned, but another part thrived on a growing consensus on what good schooling might look like. Or so it seemed to me, in that part of the public school "establishment" I found myself in.

As one of the founders of Central Park East School in New York City, I had the opportunity to work with teachers and students who modeled democracy and valued teacher and student voices. Despite the challenges of creating a school that went against the grain, I had daily victories, those wonderful, precious moments when I could see and enjoy the miracle we had created. I'd stop in the hallway and look both ways and feel such a swell of joy that it carried me over the bumps in the road. I listened to the unauditioned chorus with wonder; that's what democracy sounds like, I thought. We had created a community that was sometimes less than ideal but was always a shared cross-generational community. Parents, teachers, other staff, and students knew they were in it together. Progressive educator Lillian Weber insisted on putting her finger on the essential core principle; we needed to create adult communities of learners to tackle the issues facing us together, what we had originally called "open corridors." Lillian spoke her mind to power whenever she could and led us to cracks we hadn't dreamed existed, much less dared to test out in practice, and eventually to rebuilding hundreds of schools throughout New York City and beyond.

Today we mourn the loss of some of that work. But what I fear more would be losing the tough-minded understanding of what's needed. While we excitedly chanted the newest slogan, "This is what democracy looks like!" in Madison, Wisconsin, in the spring of 2011, or in Washington, DC, at the July 2011 Save Our Schools rally, we also realized that we don't want to slip into a simplification. Democracy is not just a rally or even a chorus. The togetherness that democracy depends on, we've learned, is far more complicated than marching or even singing together. Democracy is hard—hard to envision sometimes—and even harder to achieve. But struggle we must.

The kind of democracy we envision may be utopian, but efforts to create something closer to such an ideal are never fruitless. When I've been accused of being naive I've cringed, and yet there's truth to it. There's a kind of naïveté we dare not lose. Idealism is not a character flaw; it's a way of visualizing what could be and might be.

Schools that do not give us, our families, and our students a chance to experience the complexity of democracy—even down to such details as who should vote, and on what—deprive children of something they desperately need to learn about. Disagreements that we so carefully try to hide from the young are precisely what the young need to learn about, thoughtfully and mindfully. When we try to hide from children the complexity of creating democratic schools—when we make the struggles and the disagreements and the battles invisible—we deny young people the opportunities to understand how important and challenging this work is. Children learn most efficiently as apprentices to experts, even imperfect experts. Only when we adults accept and model the ways we wrestle with the complex challenges we struggle with—as teachers, administrators, and citizens—can our schools become places where children will learn to be responsible adults too.

What do we need now? We desperately need democratic schools. Democracy was invented as a form of accountability. By listening to and valuing every voice, we make it much more likely that we are paying attention to what's really happening and are being responsible to those with whom we interact. And democratic schools are the way to build accountability for education.

And we need resistance to the continuing assault on public education that reduces schools to market-driven factories that select and sort our students, distorting visions of communities of learning and growth and activism. We can't internalize the norm that's out there and can't accept that this is "the way things have to be." We mustn't adjust to injustice, losing our visions, our hope, and our active resistance.

One of the most powerful ways to resist the dominant, suffocating narratives that surround us—about what's wrong with schools, about blaming teachers, about the benefits of privatized education— is to create alternative images and share alternative data.

And perhaps the most persuasive forms of "alternative data" are our stories. Our lives—our lived experiences—are our data. Test scores are, at best, indirect evidence of what is happening in schools for children, but our lives and stories are the *real* data. When we sit down with a child and listen to her read, we have much more useful and powerful evidence of that child's reading skills than through viewing a test score.

This book provides us with *real* data about what market-driven educational policies have done to our students, our teachers, and our educational system. And the stories here are also the real evidence of what resistance looks like and what is possible when people work individually and collectively to teach in the cracks and to create different realities for children in schools. Corporate-driven educational initiatives undermine teachers' judgment and knowledge; they deny the most important source of data that we have, the perceptions and understandings of those closest to the action. While school improvement may be slow, to be effective it must be based on teachers', parents', and students' reality—their own understanding of the lives of children.

This book is all about stories. Stories of pain, stories of hope, stories of possibility, stories of vision, and then, perhaps most significantly, stories of activism and change. Storytelling is an art and it's the root of our literacy; this book helps us to become more literate about the world of school and the possibilities of real school change that is rooted in the real lives of children and classrooms. I believe that the stories shared in this book can open our eyes, broaden our perspectives, and engage us in powerful discussions of what is and what still can be.

In order to make things better, we need solidarity, but not a form of lockstep solidarity in which we sign on to one another's reality without close scrutiny. To work together, we need to look for the commonness between us—the places in which we can combine our gifts, our skills, and our visions to make schools truly democratic institutions that work for all students (and their teachers and their parents too).

This book helps us to be audacious in our activism, visions, and desire for audacious children who will challenge the status quo and move us forward. Gandhi said that we must be the change we wish to see in the world; in order for our children to be strategic and courageous, we must be strategic and courageous ourselves. The stories in the book help us to become the change we wish to see in the world.

At this critical time in our struggle, we need initiative, courage, imagination, and creativity. We need to believe in the value of each and every human being. And we need voices of courage.

I invite you to listen to the voices in this book and find your own courage—educational courage—to make a difference in the world.

—*Deborah Meier*

Preface

High standards? Accountability? Success for all? What could be wrong with these goals for education? Who could be against wanting all children to learn and succeed in school?

But wait! What if the ways these ideas are being articulated and enacted don't actually take us where we want to go? What if the standards that are set aren't reasonable? What if the people setting the standards don't really understand the students they're imposing the standards on? What if the teachers are being held accountable for things that keep them from reaching many other meaningful educational goals for their students? And what if the rhetoric of success for all has actually resulted in the systematic failure of large numbers of students and schools that don't have the resources that more privileged students have?

This book is about the real lives of teachers and students who have been caught in a firestorm of educational rhetoric and putative educational policies that are undermining public education and their courageous reactions to it. You will read narratives of those who have resisted what is hurtful to children and families.

This book is full of personal stories because we believe that the truth of what is happening in the schools is best represented by the words of those who are there. And, because we have asked others to share their personal stories, we begin with our own stories.

Who are we? How did we come to write this book? What educational experiences shaped our own educational philosophies and understanding of best practice?

Nancy's story depicts the powerful potential of public education, and how very different it is from what market-driven educational policies have forced public education to become today. Mara's story describes her experiences with the problematic aspects of her school experience—such as an overemphasis on competition, a narrowing of the curriculum, and useless assessments—that are hallmarks of market-driven education today.

Nancy's Story

I was fortunate to have a fourth-grade teacher who shaped my vision of what public education in a democracy could be. Mrs. Burns built a community of children where we all learned to the highest standards. For example, my classmates and I recited challenging poetry and worked together to solve tough math problems. While Mrs. Burns played the piano, she led us in spirited singing of classic songs from the 1920s to 1950s. With students, she organized recess games for the whole class, so boys weren't playing baseball while girls played hopscotch and others stood alone on the playground.

From her teaching, we learned that we could live very happily in a classroom community where we all achieved because we helped each other, respected each other despite our significant differences, worked hard, made decisions together, and experienced zest, fun, and care. In public school, we experienced a democracy and learned the possibilities for a democratic society.

When I began teaching, I sought a teaching situation where I could foster democracy through public education. Teaching primarily African American students in a large, urban high school, I integrated into my social studies curriculum African American history and current civil rights issues. I expanded my curriculum to connect to my students' lived experiences and helped them create positive visions for the future.

In the late 1960s, the Philadelphia Public Schools created a wide variety of alternative schools within the public school system. They were not charter schools that got public money without accountability, but innovative schools within the school district. I transferred to an alternative high school, collaboratively run by the school district, the University of Pennsylvania, and a local community organization. A large Victorian building housed two hundred students for whom part of the curriculum was community-based. At least one day a week, each student worked in a grassroots organization or in another local internship.

Despite the ongoing, inevitable challenges of educating young people whose families were struggling to survive, most students thrived. Poor readers learned to read when introduced to the stories of Richard Wright, students developed pride in themselves and their community, and former gang members visited colleges with their teachers and went on to enroll. This was meaningful, public education enabling our students to go on to become teachers, lawyers, community leaders, and more.

There were very few standardized tests and scripted curricula, and no merit pay in this experience of public education. I taught because I had a commitment to young people, democracy, and social change. I still teach not to create workers for corporate America but to foster the development of intelligent, critical, caring persons who can contribute to the public good in their personal and professional lives. My hope is that we can reframe and reclaim public education today for the common good.

Mara's Story

My understandings of what schools could be like—and should be like—was shaped early in my life by living and going to school in three countries before I was eight. First grade in Spain and second grade in Scotland taught me that there are many different ways to see the world, and I returned to third grade in the United States already committed to inclusion and diversity.

Although I always did well in school academically, I also realized early on that many of the ways in which schools were structured—with a focus on competition and individual achievement—stood in the way of collaborating and developing meaningful relationships. I often found myself in situations in which I had to make an active choice between "doing well" and "having friends," a choice I continue to feel no child should have to make.

When I became a teacher of a group of six- to eight-year-old students who were labeled as having "special educational needs," I saw immediately the negative results of isolating students who were perceived as different. My own isolation as "the special education teacher" also kept me from developing collaborative, cooperative relationships with other teachers. I worked hard to create a classroom in which students were encouraged to help one another and to celebrate each other's success.

My teaching experience also taught me, sadly, that many of the things that I thought were best for my students were disallowed by those in positions of power who—although they had never met my students—thought they knew better what those children needed. This experience shaped my belief in the importance of honoring teachers' knowledge and understanding of children's education. Frustrations with policies that were developed by those with minimal relationships to children and their families were clearly a barrier to achievement and the development of family and community connections.

My teaching now focuses on the importance of developing caring, safe, and nurturing communities as the essential groundwork for successful education at any level. I believe that good teaching is about building relationships, and I challenge policies and practice that damage or destroy a sense of community or collective action.

Our Collaboration

The two of us met in 1985 when we attended a conference of the International Association for the Study of Cooperation in Education. We were both passionately interested in ways to structure teaching and learning that had students work together actively and that used peer support as a primary method of instruction, preparing students to become citizens in democratic communities.

From our initial meeting, we went on to work, present, and write together, focusing our work on what we called "socially conscious cooperative learning"—cooperative learning used to help students become active agents in working for social justice and aware of the importance of their own positive interactions and support. These are the values and practices that we believe are crucial to bring back into public education today.

Nancy's Resistance Story

For the past fifteen years, I've written columns and letters in area newspapers about the dangers of high-stakes testing with examples of more effective ways to assess learning, the lack of evidence to support federal educational policy, the loss of local educational control of public education, and the undermining of multicultural education. I've worked in our union to push back against harmful educational policies and marched in Albany, New York, and Washington, DC, to preserve public education. Two stories of organized resistance stand out.

In 2000, a new superintendent in my school district sought to change the district's progressive, student-centered educational policies to ones that were authoritarian and test-based. Working together with other parents and some teachers, we organized the Education Network, a community-based group committed to educational advocacy. We held public forums on topics such as the problems with standardized testing, wrote newsletters, spoke at school board meetings, and organized others to join. Our members, including me, ran for the school board in the next few years and won seats. Our school district now has a different superintendent who does what's possible to put testing in its proper place and supports education with young people at the center.

The result of efforts to push back conservative initiatives at my own institution weren't as positive. In 2003, for example, the college president at that time eliminated much of the K–12 teacher access to a highly regarded, progressive graduate program in multicultural education. With others—students, faculty, alumni, area educators, national multicultural education leaders, and New York State teacher unions—we organized many voices to try to turn this decision around. These voices weren't heeded. We experienced a painful loss to these same ambushing policies at work in public higher education.

In both struggles, however, it was the collective effort that was most memorable. The camaraderie, cooperation, and engagement of people working together toward a common goal made our efforts meaningful and life affirming. As we work in our communities and nationwide to challenge threats to public education, whether we meet rewarding victories or intransigence, relish the journey.

Mara's Resistance Story

My resistance stories focus on attempts to address policies and practices that are discriminatory and oppressive to those in marginalized groups. A commitment to create schools that are inclusive and respond positively to difference is seriously challenged by practices that focus on ranking, competition, and attempts to reward the performances of students and teachers. When teachers are rewarded for the performances of their students, there is a serious disincentive to accept and include students who present learning and behavioral challenges.

I have also served as an expert witness in due process hearings for students and their families who are seeking more inclusion in their public schools. When a twelve-year-old student whom I'll call John entered sixth grade, all the supports and accommodations he had previously received, which had enabled him to be in a typical classroom, were removed. In the name of "high standards" and uniform curriculum, his teachers were forced to treat him "like all the other kids," which meant that he failed time and time again. It took a lawsuit (and a lot of money) for the district to acknowledge and respond to John as an individual rather than as a set of data points. In this case, as in other cases across the country, many educators, researchers, and activists have worked together collaboratively against the identification, labeling, and segregation based on test scores and worked to ensure that we see students as full and complex human beings who cannot be reduced to numbers.

In my work on addressing issues of racism and homophobia in education, I have seen, time and time again, how the current focus on high-stakes testing and a standardized curriculum has made it extremely difficult for teachers to focus on the essential community building and attention to peer interaction that is critical to student achievement and growth. Many teachers have come to me distraught that they are not allowed to address issues of bullying and racism that occur in their classrooms because test preparation has usurped their time and trumped their abilities to be thoughtful and responsive to students and school communities. In an effort to address the critical classroom climate issues these teachers raised, a group of us organized a "Teaching Respect for All" conference on our campus at Syracuse University. We were committed to sharing strategies and deepening the conversation about how to create democratic, inclusive educational programs in which all students are supported and safe. The conference drew so much interest that we had to change the venue to accommodate the teachers, administrators, parents, and students who wanted to be part of this activist strategizing.

Conclusion

By sharing our accounts of the promise and pitfalls of public education in our own experience and by sharing experiences of our resistance to market-driven education, we hope to encourage you to similarly reflect on your experiences. Our own stories can shed light on what is valuable and what is hurtful to public education. You too may have accounts of resistance to harmful policies that are the seeds of further change.

We believe that, despite the grave threat to public education today, we can collectively turn the tide. We hope the vision in this book will encourage you to hold on to hope and join with others to reclaim public education for the public good.

—*Nancy Schniedewind and Mara Sapon-Shevin*

Introduction

This book is a chronicle of courage, hope, and inspiration. It offers the voices of those who are resisting legislation, policies, and practices that are inconsistent with a democratic vision of education and society. Rather than simply lamenting what is happening in our schools, these people are actively finding ways to foster educational equity for all in the face of significant odds. Educational reformer Deborah Meier says, "Resistance to nonsense is one of the greatest powers of human beings."

The sound bites about "school reform" that we hear on the news are deceptive; the voices in this book are the real, seldom-heard accounts of those on the ground making a difference. Charts and graphs cannot tell us what it is like to teach in a kindergarten that has eliminated play, or what it is like to be forced to administer tests that you know your students cannot pass. It is through stories of the people who are in schools and communities that we can craft a picture of how education is being undermined and of how courageous people can make a difference.

This book tells stories of educators, parents, students, and community members who are individually and collectively fighting for public education that affirms young people and works for the common good. The voices here represent hundreds of thousands of others who continue to protest the policies that have damaged millions of young people and that have the potential to destroy public education. We hope this book encourages those who value public education to speak up and push policymakers in democratic directions. We hope readers will be able to envision and support alternatives to what is and work to transform current educational and other social policies and practices into those that nourish all young people.

The purpose of public education in a democracy is to provide a meaningful, challenging, and equitable education for all students, one that sets high academic expectations without regard to race, class, gender, family of origin, or language. Equally important is that students learn to participate in a democratic society and work with people different from themselves. We imagine schools in which students view one another as vital resources and understand that a successful society is one in which no person is discarded or disenfranchised. We work for diverse, inclusive school environments where thoughtfulness, care, and cooperation help prepare students to be critical thinkers, problem solvers, and active participants in their local and broader communities.

Educational policies driven by market concerns ambush the possibility for this kind of democratic education. High-stakes testing, voucher programs, corporate-connected charter schools, test-driven teacher evaluation, merit pay, mayoral control, and national standards put private corporations at the helm of education, rather than the public. Our educational system is being privatized and, in the process, our democracy is threatened.

The Educational Courage of Resisters

This book describes the reality of public schools and presents the stories of those who have had the courage to resist market-driven policies and practices from the initiation of No Child Left Behind (NCLB) in 2002 to 2011. The voices in the book reflect different kinds of resistance, with people saying no in a variety of ways. While some spend their energy working within the system to provide meaningful education for young people, others concurrently take actions to resist them. Still others focus their energy on organizing collective activity to challenge ambushing practices at the local, state, and national levels. Many integrate all these approaches.

Part I, "Is This What We Call 'Education'?" includes a history of the current ambush of public education and the effects of ill-considered federal legislation on young people, educators, parents, and communities. A teacher and parent describe what has happened to their teaching and to young people because of these policies and courageously dissent in a time characterized by conformity and fear. These accounts can help raise consciousness about the reality of schools today, a necessary place to start a movement for change.

The voices in part II, " 'I Won't Be a Part of This!'—Educators, Parents, Students, and Community Members Resist," represent many thousands of other people across the country who, as individuals and small groups, have resisted the current, top-down educational agenda. Some resist by writing op-ed pieces; some publicly say no by refusing to take a test or resigning from a charter school that has "gone corporate." Others resist by organizing neighbors to change testing policies detrimental to English-language learners. By refusing to be silent, this group of writers gives courage to others who may think about similar actions.

"Resisting by 'Working in the Cracks'—Creating Spaces to Teach Authentically," part III, describes how educators, even when constrained, create space within the current system to teach authentically. Committed to developing students' intellectual, social, and emotional learning, they explain how they foster socially just classrooms and schools and keep their teaching vibrant and curriculum relevant despite test-driven constraints. An encouraging account from one public alternative school, included on the *Educational Courage* website (www.beacon.org/educationalcourage), shows that "choice" for students and families is possible without the privatizing demands of charter schools. These stories of creativity, resilience, and perseverance will inspire other educators to find the cracks in their own educational settings where they can teach with young people at the center.

" 'Not My Voice Alone'—Organizing to Reclaim Public Education," part IV, presents ways in which students, educators, parents, and community members have articulated alternative visions for public education and fought for meaningful change. Whether they're resisting paying teachers for test scores, organizing against charter school takeovers, fighting mayoral control, or educating others about the dangers of a business model of education, these examples of organized, public resistance encourage others to reclaim a sense of urgency in fighting for public education. Contributors also describe the work of local and national organizations that have built coalitions for broader outreach and advocacy. Writers present a vision of ways we can act together toward progressive, multicultural, and democratic schools as we move into the future.

Even more voices of resilience and courage are found on the *Educational Courage* website. Coordinated with the book sections, pieces there offer powerful stories from others who fight for public education. In addition, the *Educational Courage* website contains practical materials related to the narratives in the book. Fact sheets from the National Center for Fair and Open Testing (FairTest) and Parents United for Responsible Education (PURE), for example, provide excellent examples of materials that educate others. There are also resource lists of organizations and materials, a bibliography, and contributor biographies.

The pieces in *Educational Courage* are organized by theme rather than chronologically. The sequence builds from understanding school realities, to stories of individual resistance, to accounts of meaningful teaching despite top-down constraints, and finally to narratives of organized, collective resistance. A chronology of the creeping assault on public education from the passage of NCLB in 2002 to 2011—"A Short History of the Ambush of Public Education"—introduces part I. A snapshot of the movement to protest against these policies, provided next, gives context to the voices of the resisters whose stories you'll read in *Educational Courage.*

A Decade of Educational Activism

Ever since the ambush of public education began, there have been educators, parents, and students who have spoken up to protest these hurtful policies. While market-driven initiatives began to threaten public education during the Reagan administration, they became solidly institutionalized in federal educational policy with the passage of NCLB. While people have spoken out to counter these policies over the past thirty years, this book focuses on the decade since 2002.

Well before NCLB, organizations and individuals were advocating for progressive, democratic education. Some like the North

Dakota Study Group focused on building democratic classrooms and schools and critiqued narrow methods of accountability and assessments. Others like the National Coalition of Educational Activists, a multiracial organization of parents, teachers, child advocates, union, and community activists, connected educational advocacy to broader struggles for social justice, equality, and democracy in order to improve public education.

Founded by Milwaukee teachers and parents in 1985, *Rethinking Schools* magazine became a voice not only for those doing meaningful social justice education in their schools, but for those resisting policies that undercut educational equity. *Rethinking Schools* continues to link classroom issues to policy concerns and chronicles the activism of teachers, parents, and students fighting for quality education for all children. Its superb books and curricula support educators working to enable students to achieve academically and act democratically.

In the late 1990s, more resisters sounded the alarm about the dangers of standardizing education. Susan Ohanian wrote the influential *One Size Fits Few: The Folly of Educational Standards* in 1999 and has been writing about the dangers of testing and the privatization of public education ever since. In the same year, George N. Schmidt, a well-respected veteran teacher, was fired from his twenty-eight-year teaching job in Chicago when he published samples of the Chicago Academic Standards Examinations (CASE) in his journal *Substance*. He continues to critique the effects of harmful educational policies in *Substance News*. The National Center for Fair and Open Testing—FairTest—began its work to end the misuses and flaws of standardized testing and to ensure that evaluation of students, teachers, and schools is fair, open, valid, and educationally beneficial. FairTest continues to provide excellent information, technical assistance and advocacy on a broad range of testing concerns.

After the passage of NCLB, awareness of the problems with standardized testing and federal control over educational policy began to grow. Parents, like those whose stories follow, fought the negative effects of testing on their children and schools all across the country throughout the decade. More recently, parent groups like Class Size Matters in New York City have fought overcrowding, corporate-connected charter schools, mayoral control, and the privatizing of education. In 2010, parent groups across the country joined together in Parents Across America in an effort to bring their voices into educational policymaking on national, as well as local and state levels.

Teachers have organized in their unions to fight for progressive educational policies. Some formed caucuses within large city unions, such as in Los Angeles, to resist corporate charter takeovers of schools and standardized testing. The Caucus of Rank and File Educators (CORE) in Chicago won the 2010 election to lead the Chicago Teachers Union, and Bob Peterson, *Rethinking Schools* editor and advocate of social justice unionism, was elected president of the Milwaukee Teachers' Education Association in 2011. Some groups like the Grassroots Education Movement (GEM) in New York City work both within and outside the larger teacher unions to educate and organize teachers, parents, students, and communities against corporate and government policies that underfund and privatize public schools. GEM produced the outstanding documentary, *The Inconvenient Truth behind Waiting for Superman* to further expose these policies.

Teachers have formed progressive organizations in various areas across the country to give each other encouragement, to share teaching strategies that support social justice, and to fight policies that undermine public education. These teacher activist groups across the country also typically hold annual conferences in various cities. In his piece in *Educational Courage,* contributor Sam Coleman describes the way the New York Collective of Radical Educators (NYCoRE) supported his successful school-based effort to resist merit pay.

Throughout the past decade, numerous educators have written about the impending threat to public education. Among them are longtime democratic educator Deborah Meier and Diane Ravitch, former assistant secretary of education, whose dialogue, "Bridging Differences," has been published in *Education Week* since 2007. Once an advocate of school choice, testing, and accountability, Ravitch published her influential *The Death and Life of the Great American School System* in 2010, arguing that these very policies are hurting students, teachers, and public education.

As the ambush of public education has become more intense, activism has increased. *Rethinking Schools* posted the "Not Waiting for Superman" website where critics responded to the myths underlying the corporate-supported film *Waiting for Superman* and generated ideas for local protests and actions that germinated across the country. When Governor Scott Walker tried to fast-track a bill to strip Wisconsin teachers and other public employees of their bargaining rights, Madison became a center of Wisconsin protest and national solidarity.

Civil rights groups have challenged the way market-driven educational policies harm students of color. In 2010, a coalition of groups, including the NAACP, the Lawyers' Committee for Civil Rights Under Law, and Rainbow/PUSH Coalition, criticized Race to the Top legislation for emphasizing competitive incentives that leave the majority of low-income and students of color behind. It also critiqued the shutting down of low-performing schools, rather than doing more to close gaps in resources and to end racial segregation in schools. The coalition's report pressed for policy changes because "for too long communities of color have been testing grounds for unproven methods of educational change." In 2011, the NAACP Legal Defense Fund and FairTest, among others, critiqued NCLB for catalyzing the school-to-prison pipeline. They documented how high-stakes testing and zero-tolerance policies have pushed students out of school into the juvenile and criminal justice systems, with especially severe effects on students of color and students with disabilities.

Students have also fought vigorously for their public schools. For example, students in Raza Studies Program in the Tucson High

Magnet School chained themselves to the empty chairs belonging to school board members to deter a vote that could close down their culturally relevant and academically successful program. In the spring of 2011, students at the Catherine Ferguson Academy in Detroit, a public school for pregnant students and young mothers, were handcuffed and arrested after sitting down in front of their very successful school to protest its imminent closure.

Moving Forward

The future holds the hope of new directions in the fight for public education, including more national organizing, growing social justice unionism, and assertive public actions. Thousands of educators, parents, students, and administrators from across the country marched to keep public schools "public" at the Save Our Schools march in Washington, DC, in July 2011. Educators committed to principles of social justice unionism, such as those in Los Angeles and Milwaukee, are building coalitions with diverse communities to enlarge a base for awareness and activism. Young people and adults alike, making more bold public protests, are willing to risk arrest to call attention to the injustices that threaten public education. From the local to national level, from individual protests to collective civil disobedience, advocates of public education are developing creative approaches to educate and organize. Since social inequality and privatization also ambush the economy, housing, the health-care system, and the media, it will take a broad movement to foster the social change that is needed to revive democratic schooling in a democratic society.

Bolstered by the many examples in this volume and on the *Educational Courage* website, we hold out the hope that educators, students, and parents can *concurrently* forge strategies for surviving and thriving within the system *and* also use their individual and collective power to critique and challenge the many policies and practices that undermine public education today. The narratives here show that there's no one way to resist and that courage, resilience, and organization are core values. We hope these accounts show the wide range of possibility for transforming "what is" into "what can be."

Margaret Mead, in a famous quote, said, "Never doubt that a small group of concerned citizens can make a difference. Indeed, it is the only thing that ever has." We must begin with a shared conviction that change is possible; we must become informed and work together from a place of solidarity not only to resist but to sustain and create alternative spaces and visions for public education and a democratic society. This book is designed to help us on that journey.

Part I

Introduction: "Is This What We Call 'Education'?"

What is your vision of a "good education"? Whether our own schooling was primarily positive or damaging, most of us have an idea of what meaningful education should be. Despite differences in educational philosophies or experiences, many of us probably share a common core of hopes for the education of our children and the children of this nation.

When you picture a "good education," do you see young people working hard, sharing ideas, engaging with each other, and learning information and skills that will enable them to contribute productively to our society as adults? Do you see students who are challenged, striving to reach their fullest potential, and provided with the support they need? Do you imagine caring and affirming relationships between everyone in the classroom and school? Can you imagine, in Deborah Meier's words, schools where "there is no harm done"? Public education has never consistently provided a quality education for all young people, but as market-driven policymakers have gained more power, we see less of this vision alive in schools today. The imprints of federal and corporate initiatives may be felt less in predominantly white and more economically privileged communities, but they are there, and many parents are saddened by the amount of time that goes into test preparation and test taking. Districts that have developed strong educational track records based on years of hard work building successful child-centered educational programs find their autonomy eroded. Local control of education, a time-honored principle in our democracy, is being whittled away.

The impact of these policies on urban communities is much more severe. Scripted curricula deny teachers their creativity, and narrow educational goals make implementing multicultural initiatives and an enriched curriculum very difficult. Under mayoral control in some cities, a segregated, hierarchical system of education has developed, with charter schools taking over parts of functioning public schools and receiving more resources and space. In New York City, for example, some charter school operators accepted only students who had high test scores. In a school shared by charter and public school children, the public school students didn't have direct access to school entrances or the shared lunchroom and gym because they weren't allowed to walk through the charter school section. Is this equal education?

Some people have protested the imposition of top-down, market-driven policies by setting up mock graveyards in which each gravestone depicts something that has disappeared from public education. Arts-based curriculum, local control of education, recess, parental input—these mock graveyards overflowed with epitaphs to commemorate what was valued and now has been lost in public education.

"A Short History of the Ambush of Public Education" describes the difference between a public, democratic approach to education and the corporate-driven approach that's been central to federal educational policy since the implementation of No Child Left Behind in 2002, and chronicles the growth of these initiatives over the past decade. The voices of a teacher and a parent follow, vividly describing the effects of these policies on young people, teachers, and families.

Susan Hobart, the author of "One Teacher's Cry," describes the loss of her passion for teaching when practices she *knows* are effective with students have suddenly been deemed inappropriate because of new policies. Susan writes, "I was recently told we cannot buddy up with a first-grade class during our core literacy time. It does not fit the definition of core literacy, I was told. Reading with younger children has been a boon to literacy improvement for my struggling readers and my new English-speaking students. Now I must throw this tool away?"

In "Rachel's Plea," mother and teacher Wendy Goodman describes the tragic results of a ten-year-old child's struggle with test anxiety: "Fourth-grade nervous breakdowns should never occur. She cries to be able just to be a kid." Is this what we call "education"?

The theme that emerges in these narratives is the loss of hope. By seeing the reality of classrooms and schools from a human perspective, we can gain the knowledge and empathy to say, "Enough!" We hope these accounts will open your minds and hearts to the human consequences of current educational "de-form." Acknowledgment of the depth of the losses can motivate passion for change.

1. A Short History of the Ambush of Public Education

Nancy Schniedewind

While some Americans already see how privatization is ambushing public schools, many believe that market-driven initiatives will improve and save our public schools. How can we understand the erosion of public education since the No Child Left Behind Act, in particular? By comparing the ideas of market-driven education to those of democratic, public education, while also looking at the federal educational policies of the past decade as a bigger picture, the ambush of public education becomes clearer.

The Creeping Changes in Public Education

During the 1960s and 1970s, at the time of the civil rights movement and the women's liberation movement, social programs were created to address poverty and create greater equality in society. A growing commitment to equality, inclusion, and respect for diversity spawned programs of racial desegregation, bilingual education, multicultural education, and the beginning of a strong movement to include students with disabilities in public schools with their nondisabled peers evidenced. As the desire for equality in society was clearly articulated and embraced, the racial achievement gap in schools was the smallest in recent history.

However, since the Reagan administration, there has been a creeping ambush of public education. Until recently, attacks on democratic goals and policies for public education were largely concealed, with the rhetoric of high-stakes testing, vouchers, charter schools, and business involvement in education couched in appealing terms. But the realities of these policies paint a different picture. The 2002 federal No Child Left Behind (NCLB) Act is a case in point. Who would want to leave any child behind? Yet this very legislation has resulted in the dropout, push-out, or failure of hundreds of thousands of students.

This ambush of public education is directly tied to the growth of neoliberal economic, social, and educational policies—market-driven policies that attempt to transfer control of resources away from the public sector to the private sector, promoting profit over other social goals. The market-driven policies of politicians, economists, and corporate leaders that deregulate the economy, liberalize trade, and dismantle public services by privatizing them have become more entrenched since the 1980s.

The neoliberal goal for education is ostensibly to give students the skills and knowledge they need to be productive workers. Yet, the level of education their practices support prepares most students for mechanistic, low-paying jobs. It supports education policies such as NCLB and Race to the Top (RTTT) that allow failing schools to be administered by private corporations or converted to charter schools. These policies have also led to funding private schools through voucher programs and the significant expansion of corporate-connected charter schools. Within a market-driven framework, schooling as a public good is under attack. We are told that "private" is good and "public" is bad.

The problem is not only the decisions that are made, but how those decisions are made. Neoliberalism transforms the nature and quality of community discussion. People think less about democracy and a commitment to community and the common good, and think instead about democracy as the individual choosing within a competitive marketplace. Instead of asking, "What do *we* want from our public schools for all children?" people are encouraged to ask, "Which school should I choose for *my* child?"

Market-driven educational policies erode democratic ideals and practices and are not "reforms" that promise positive change for all children. The real reformers are people like the contributors to this collection. This book will show that those who are committed to democratic public education, while cast by neoliberals as *preservers* of the status quo, are the true reformers.

What Are the Basic Tenets of the Market-Driven Ideology
That Ambush Public Education?

Public schools are failing: Educators are to blame
Corporate-driven policymakers hold educators and parents completely responsible for "failing schools" and the learning problems of students, without any attention to out-of-school factors such as poverty.

Public school advocates show us that it is public policy that is failing our schools. Poverty, inadequate health care, unemployment, substandard housing, resegregation, and food insecurity all greatly affect young people's ability to learn. And are public schools really failing? While the media consistently portray how bad schools are, poor performance is mostly due to the much higher level of poverty in the United States compared to other nations. For example, on the latest international test, the Program for International Student Assessment (PISA), American schools in which fewer than 10 percent of the students were poor outperformed the schools of the highest-performing nations. As the proportion of poor students rises, the scores of U.S. schools drop.[1] While there are certainly many changes needed in our public schools, in fact, most Americans give their local public schools good grades.

High-stakes testing makes public schools accountable
Corporate-driven policies assume that accountability requires high-stakes, standardized tests so that policymakers and administrators can use classroom, school, and district scores to reward or punish teachers and assess school quality. They claim that such testing shines a light on failing schools.

Democratic reformers know that high-stakes testing is unfair to many students, including students in poorly funded schools, those whose first language is not English, and those who suffer test anxiety. Such one-size-fits-all testing narrows the curriculum to those subjects that will be tested, often measuring low-level thinking while failing to assess high-level learning. Rather, we need to promote multiple types of assessments that respond to the needs and experiences of diverse students. These more effectively encourage and measure student achievement and hold schools accountable.

The goal of education is competition in the global marketplace
Neoliberals want schools to produce students who can help U.S. businesses better compete internationally, shifting the focus from child development to business gains. As writer Jonathan Kozol points out, this view sees children as economic units or products, as exemplified in the mission statement of one Ohio elementary school: "We aim to produce workers who will sharpen America's edge in the global marketplace."

Public school reformers insist that young people are not commodities, but children, and education is not a product, but a process with the goal of preparing students intellectually and socially to become economically sufficient and engaged participants in a democratic society. As the editors of *Rethinking Schools* remind us, "There are many non-market (perhaps even anti-market) purposes for learning: to end wars, to effect racial equality, to curb greenhouse gases, to halt domestic violence, to appreciate the arts, to play sports and exercise . . . and to learn to live together."[2]

The private sector can better manage our schools
Neoliberals argue that education will show more success if it is run by the private sector, not the public sector, using business models that are data-driven to make schools more efficient. Neoliberals see public education as a market to be privatized through charter schools, voucher programs, and the expanding power of testing companies, corporations, and hedge fund investors. Unions, impediments to privatization, are intentionally undermined and discredited.

Democratic reformers insist that schools aren't businesses and should maintain the legacy of local control to serve the public good. When flourishing, schools are communities of care and cooperation where students learn and grow in unique and complex ways and where teachers are valued for their professional skills. Unions are valued for protecting educators' rights and fostering positive educational change based on well-tested practices.

Market-Driven Policies at Work: NCLB and Its Legacy

The market-driven ideas and policies at the core of NCLB remain at the heart of federal education policies today. NCLB required all states receiving federal funds to establish learning standards in reading, math, and other subjects; to create standardized tests and proficiency levels to measure student progress; and to make annual yearly progress (AYP) so that all students would be proficient in reading and math by 2014. Schools that didn't make AYP faced increasingly strong consequences, including "restructuring," which could mean becoming a charter school, firing school staff, privatizing, or being taken over by the state. In 2011, U.S. Secretary of Education Arne Duncan offered the states optional "waivers" to the failed AYP; however, the waivers required even more reliance on test score data for accountability. This flawed approach didn't increase the capacity of schools to improve educational services, especially when test scores largely reflect the poverty, inequality, and segregation of their student populations. *Rethinking Schools* editor Stan Karp commented that it's like passing out thermometers in a malaria epidemic when people really need better health care and medicine.

Since NCLB tied impossible demands and no resources to punitive sanctions, and assumed an equal playing field when there was none, it was destined to demolish the public schools. Jonathan Kozol pointed out how hypocritical it is for members of Congress and the president to hold third graders accountable on standardized tests when most of them aren't provided the resources their own children have, such as preschool education. No other area—housing, health care, or child poverty—faces such demands, under the threat of sanctions, for equality among population groups within twelve years. Stan Karp wrote, "Imagine a federal law that declared that 100 percent of all citizens must have adequate health care in twelve years or sanctions will be imposed on doctors and hospitals. Or all crime must be eliminated in twelve years or the local police department will face privatization."[3]

What Are the Consequences of Corporate-Driven Educational Policies?

Two overarching consequences of NCLB and subsequent corporate-based policies are: the public perception that public schools are failing; and the local communities' loss of control over public schools. Rather than promote school improvement or accountability, the perception that the system has failed is eroding our common belief in the value of a universal system of public education, a value that is intrinsic to its survival.

Until recently, the federal government was involved in education only to promote access and equity, such as through school desegregation and programs for special needs and poor children. But market-based federal policy that promotes test-driven, top-down "standards and accountability" for all U.S. schools discredits public education and funds school privatization. Since 2009, Secretary Duncan has greatly expanded the federal government's centralized power through Race to the Top, which requires states to compete for grants that encourage the development of charter schools, adopt national common standards and tests, and tie teacher evaluation to test scores.

There are many specific consequences of such policies on the real lives of teachers, students, and parents. The news media's sound bites about "failing schools," "educational reform," and "holding teachers accountable" *don't* provide real information about the following outcomes of corporate-driven education.

Schools narrow both the curriculum and accountability measures, pressuring teachers to teach to the test

In order to have students do well on tests, many school districts cut back on subjects that aren't tested, like art, music, and social studies, and expect teachers to narrowly focus their teaching on what will be on the tests. Rather than using multiple sources to assess learning, students are promoted and graduated, and entire school districts are often "graded," according to just a few tests. In addition, assessment has been taken out of the hands of local educators and imposed by state or federal policy, contradicting quality assessment practices.

Excellent teachers leave the profession
Neoliberal initiatives systematically undercut the personal and professional knowledge of educators and force teachers to implement curriculum and employ pedagogy that may directly contradict their own understanding and beliefs about education and the students they teach. Imagine trying to parent when the instructions on what to do every day with your child come from someone who has never met your child. Constrained and controlled by the requirements of standardized testing and control of the curriculum, many excellent teachers have left the profession rather than distort their own teaching.

The following quotes from teachers evidence the ways their professionalism has been undermined:

> I yearned for a creative community of learners; conference days where things weren't assigned from the top, but where I could work together with my colleagues; the ability to use my skills and not have imposed lesson plans. I gave up a lot of money to retire. It's a top down system where teachers don't have power. I wanted to return to the time when I had real responsibility.

> I'm a thinking person. Now I'm not asked to think as part of my job. I'm passionately committed to good education and I'm left out of the loop of educational decision-making. People who are closest to students aren't asked for their opinions. Those things associated with job satisfaction have disappeared.

Young people are hurt

The psychological costs of test-driven educational policies are striking, with millions of students experiencing fear, anger, and pain from the constant pressures to do well on the tests. One educator reported, for example, that students bring their rosaries to the tests and, when rubbing them, get bloody hands because they're so upset. Less visible is how students lose opportunities to develop critical thinking, creative problem solving, and social and emotional skills.

Students drop out and are pushed out

The mandate to ensure that students become proficient on tests, with no requirement that they graduate, creates an incentive to encourage students to drop out. When students don't pass the tests (sometimes several times), they "age out" or drop out, so high-stakes testing operates as a giant "push-out program," allowing a school's performance rating to rise. This occurs, in particular, with low-income students and students of color as well as students receiving special education services and English-language learners who often find the required tests completely impossible. The tests, combined with zero-tolerance policies, feed the school-to-prison pipeline, a process in which desperate young people without a high school education or a job turn to crime to survive and become part of the expansive prison system.

Race and class discrimination increases

Corporate-driven educational policies play out very differently in poor urban schools than in wealthy suburban districts. Students in many poor schools receive a system-scripted curriculum and limited educational offerings, while those in wealthy schools get enriched curricula and more innovative instructional strategies. NCLB and other test-driven policies represent a diminished vision of civil rights. Educational equity is reduced to equalizing test scores. The effect has been to impoverish the educational experience of students of color and to reinforce the two-tier system of public education that civil rights advocates once challenged.

A business model is taking over education,
and private corporations are making huge profits
Expanding options for privatizing education include reopening a "failing" school as a charter school managed by an outside organization that creates a market for supplemental educational services. Schools to be "turned around" often contract with for-profit firms to supply books, supplies, and "coaching" for teachers. Numerous test-prep and tutoring services make huge profits for corporations that make and often score the tests, resulting in even greater profit.

Results?
Many reports and studies indicate that market-driven policies have not improved education. Virtually all National Assessment of Educational Progress (NAEP) scores, federally funded achievement tests often referred to as the nation's report card, have dropped since the implementation of NCLB, compared to the rate of improvement for the five or so years *before* NCLB. Despite billions of dollars poured into testing companies, scripted reading curriculum, and state standards, market-driven policies have been unable to produce significant improvements on reading and math tests. In addition, closing the achievement gap between black and brown students and white students has stagnated under NCLB.

From Ambush to Onslaught
Subsequent federal policies continue to undermine public education, but in a more direct and forceful way. In 2009, Secretary Duncan, supported by corporate-based organizations like the Business Roundtable, U.S. Chamber of Commerce, and Democrats for Education Reform, as well as entrepreneurial foundations like the Bill & Melinda Gates Foundation, the Walton Family Foundation, and the Broad Foundation, pushed a well-organized and well-funded agenda for more charter schools, pay for test scores, evaluation of educators using student test scores, national curriculum standards/testing, and turnarounds for low-performing schools. Rather than helping all states and all children, Race to the Top and other federal education

policies of the Obama administration pit states against each other, bribing them to change their policies in hopes of winning millions of dollars in federal funding and reinforcing market-driven competitive values. This unprecedented degree of top-down, federal intrusion into time-honored, democratic decision-making practices for public education is the result of Department of Education regulations that didn't need congressional approval.

Although President Obama pronounced that competition for RTTT funds would not be based on politics or ideology but on "what works," none of these market-driven initiatives are backed by either solid educational research or track records. With no credible basis in research, they just happen to be, as Diane Ravitch noted, the programs and approaches favored by those in power. The Obama administration also claims that there will be no rewards for failure. Here "rewards" mean funding, and "failure" means those schools educating primarily poor children and English-language learners who don't score as well as others on standardized tests. Thus, those needing the most educational resources will get the least, which undermines a fundamental idea of American education—that public education should provide equal educational opportunity for all children.

This contrasts starkly with the best-performing educational systems that advocate neither choice nor competition as key drivers of educational improvement. Finland, for example, one of the world's top educational performers, focuses on equity and cooperation and not choice and competition to ensure that all students learn well.

What Are Current Hallmarks of Market-Driven Education?

Charter schools

Charter schools are elementary or secondary schools paid for with public money and freed from some of the rules and regulations that apply to other public schools. The privatization of public education through charter schools often passes beneath our radar because many charter schools sell themselves as "public," while their admissions' policies and requirements often mimic many private schools. While some charter schools are not-for-profit, most are run by private employment management organizations (EMOs). Even many of those that are not-for-profit are connected to and supported by for-profit corporations and hedge funds.

Although charters differ from state to state, most are defined not as public entities but as "educational corporations." While claiming to be public, charters typically educate a tiny percent of the community, including fewer English-language learners, students with special needs, and students who qualify for free lunch than do their public school counterparts. They are more racially segregated, and some find ways to push out students who don't meet test-score expectations.

The rationale for the development of charter schools was to provide places for innovations that would be transferred to public schools, but this hasn't happened and is not necessary. Since the late 1960s, alternative public schools, governed by public school districts and staffed by unionized, certified teachers, have provided spaces for curriculum innovation and alternate forms of pedagogy. Public alternative schools could be expanded. Rather, charter schools have been imposed as the only alternative, even though charters have a very mixed record of improving student achievement. A comprehensive study in 2009 by Stanford University's Center for Research on Education Outcomes found that only 17 percent of charter schools reported academic gains that were significantly better than comparable traditional public schools; 37 percent showed scores that were worse than their public school counterparts; and 46 percent showed no significant difference. Nevertheless, corporate-based spokespeople and government policymakers push charter schools as the only option for educational innovation and choice.

Charter schools reflect other problems as well. While some charter schools champion community involvement, democratic governance, and open access, many serve a select student body and prohibit teacher unions; some issue contracts that allow them to fire teachers at the will of the management, with no due process. Charter school teachers are 230 percent more likely to leave the profession than public school teachers. In some cities, charter schools privatize public space by taking over public school buildings and undermining some of the last vestiges of community space. Despite these problems, in 2010 Secretary Duncan insisted that, to successfully compete for RTTT and other federal funds, states must remove caps on the number of charter schools, not restrict student enrollment, and should provide charters with public funding for facilities. These initiatives aim to get rid of public-sector unions and turn public schools into private schools funded by public dollars.

The push for charter schools is based on the notion that competition between schools will improve education. Any system based on competition will have winners and losers, and in such a structure, when one school succeeds, another fails. Rather, what public education *should* promise is a system in which all children and schools can excel.

Paying teachers for test scores

Paying teachers for test scores, commonly misnamed "merit pay," is a system that compensates teachers and principals based on the academic gains of their students as measured by standardized tests. Neoliberals argue that if schools are managed as private companies and we reward and punish teachers on the basis of how much students learn, teachers will do better and students will learn more. RTTT guidelines encourage states to set up evaluation systems that compensate educators when their students make significant gains in primarily test-assessed academic achievement. Some systems that pay teachers for test scores directly set colleagues against each other; others adversely affect relationships by positioning teachers who should be collaborative into competitive relationships within their schools. Pay for performance can also reduce motivation and overall productivity.

While all teachers deserve pay commensurate with professionals in other fields, most teachers go into teaching because of their desire to work with young people and foster their learning, not because of the money. Rather than providing support for real learning, reward programs encourage a greater test-score focus and can discourage teachers and schools from wanting to teach students whose scores may not be high. There is little evidence that pay-for-performance systems work for people in any profession. A 2010 Vanderbilt University study showed that paying teachers for test scores does not produce higher test scores for students.[4]

Evaluating educators based on student test scores
Corporate-driven educational advocates push "data-based" policies for teacher and principal accountability, often using a value-added model (VAM) to judge educators' performance, and those of their teacher education programs, by how much their students improve (or not) on standardized tests. Under RTTT guidelines, states can't have any laws *against* linking individual student test scores to individual teachers, making student test-score growth a significant factor in the new evaluation systems. A National Research Council report confirmed, however, what multiple studies show: standardized test scores do not adequately measure student learning.

Wayne Au, an editor at *Rethinking Schools,* clarifies some of the many reasons: To begin with, there is a statistical error rate of 35 percent when using one year's worth of test data to measure a teacher's effectiveness, and an error rate of 25 percent when using data from three years. Consider also that tests scores of students taught by the same teacher fluctuate wildly from year to year. Day-to-day score instability also raises concern about VAM. Fifty to 80 percent of any improvement or decline in a student's standardized test scores can be attributed to one-time, randomly occurring factors such as having breakfast or not or having an argument on the way to school.

Whether students are tracked or segregated based on race, class, or language acquisition also greatly influences these results. Finally, other influences unrelated to school—access to health care, hunger and poverty-related stress—significantly affect student scores negatively. There are many accurate and fair approaches for assessing teacher and teacher education program effectiveness, approaches that would not require new investments in data systems, new assessments and major expansions of testing in schools.[5]

Some states' evaluation systems tie student test scores to teacher compensation or create a bell-curve evaluation system that necessitates some teachers automatically be deemed "ineffective." Under such conditions, collaboration among teachers is replaced by competition, and when this happens, every student loses.

National curriculum standards and national tests

Arguing that tougher tests will improve student learning, the Department of Education pushed for national standards aligned with common tests, requiring that states applying for RTTT participate. The national committee developing the Common Core Standards, however, included no classroom teachers and was dominated by people who work for the big test publishers.

Public school advocates raise concern that local school districts and states are losing control of education to testing companies that, with very little accountability, are determining the future of our schools while gleaning huge profits. Furthermore, a national exam will not solve the problem of teaching to the test and narrowing the curriculum.

It is very difficult, if not impossible, for national tests to be culturally relevant. Authentic, useful testing involves criteria that relate to students' experiences, points of view, and language. Will a rural child in Iowa have the same life experiences or knowledge as an urban New Yorker? Two strengths of our democratic society are its creativity and diversity; making everyone meet the same standard undermines those strengths. Nations with centralized standards generally tend to perform no better or worse on international tests than those without them. Instead of testing students based on national standards, evaluations of learning based on actual student work, low-stakes use of a very limited amount of standardized tests, and a school quality review process result in higher-quality learning and improved assessment.

Turnaround schools and mayoral control

Schools whose students score poorly on standardized tests are considered low performing and subject to turnaround policies. Aggressive interventions include closures, firing of staff, and various forms of state and private takeover. When schools are turned over to charter operators and educational entrepreneurs, they provide a new market to those who can show little track record of success in improving schools. This is especially true in urban areas, where the Department of Education encourages mayoral control of schools with little opportunity for public involvement and governance, something suburban schools still have.

Mayors who have closed neighborhood schools in low-income communities of color often destabilize already fragile communities by taking away what is sometimes the only major institution in the neighborhood. Students are often moved to unfamiliar neighborhoods or "disappear." Under mayoral control, charter schools have taken over public school buildings, often pushing out the original teachers and students. This continues despite the fact that charter students, especially African American students in cities such as Chicago and New York, have shown little or no gains on the NAEP or state tests.

Behind this situation is a story of disinvestment in urban schools for the past thirty years, a system of segregated and unequal schools that are now labeled "underperforming." Rather than close them down, we could reverse the budgets cuts and unfair tax formulas that have spawned them and provide funds for school improvement and accountability to school leaders, teachers, and parents.

Abandoning multicultural education

While corporate-backed policies ostensibly aim to close the achievement gap, their solutions emphasize sameness. The curriculum and teaching approaches they support, as Professor Christine Sleeter points out, are based on the language, worldview, and experiences of white English speakers.[6] Multicultural education, in contrast, provides culturally responsive teaching that engages students in critical thinking, active learning, and culturally relevant curricula and processes. Multicultural educators appreciate their students' social identities and attend to issues of race, gender, class, language, religion, and ability. They teach diverse students successfully because they pay attention to the context of their students' lives.

In the 1970s and 1980s, the focus in American schools on multicultural education contributed to closing the achievement gap. Market-driven educational policies have undermined multicultural education, and, instead of recognizing how institutional discrimination limits learning and creates an opportunity gap, neoliberals blame teachers.

Attacks on teachers, teacher unions, and collective bargaining
The combined public relations clout of the Gates, Broad, and Walton foundations and hedge-funded advocacy groups like Democrats for Education Reform have generated a massive crusade against teachers and teacher unions. In 2011, for example, this included a cover story in *Newsweek*, a weeklong series on NBC that celebrated the privatization and scapegoating of teachers, and two segments of *Oprah* devoted to *Waiting for Superman*, a biased documentary that blamed teachers and teacher unions for school failure.

One goal of a market-driven approach to education is to deprofessionalize the teaching profession, and its pay, by making teaching a routinized job rather than a field that requires a comprehensive education and ongoing professional development. Rather than being public intellectuals who teach young people how to think critically, solve problems creatively, and engage deeply with ideas, teachers will only need to follow a scripted curriculum geared toward passing standardized tests. Teachers will be trained quickly, paid little, and burn out, thus maintaining a revolving door of educators. Low salaries will help cut costs. But teacher unions are in the way, so neoliberals have mounted a massive public relations campaign claiming that they are an impediment to reform.

Quality education, teacher unions, and collective bargaining go hand in hand. In states where collective bargaining for educators is not allowed, effectively prohibiting teacher unions, students have the lowest scores on the SATs and ACTs, tests many colleges use for admission. And in Finland, the country with the highest-achieving students internationally, one advantage is that teachers are unionized. Furthermore, there is forward movement in some teacher unions to fairly address the issue of ineffective teachers and to develop closer ties with local communities to collaboratively work for quality education.

The influence of corporations and
entrepreneurial foundations on public education
The free-market doctrine has shifted focus away from improving how students learn to making wide profit margins for testing corporations and educational entrepreneurs. While educators have long identified problems with schools, especially urban schools, it was only when corporations saw the potential of using tax dollars for profit that businesses and hedge funds began pushing their agenda for public education.

States now spend five to six times more on tests than they did before NCLB, with most funds going to testing companies. Pearson, a testing company that creates "data systems that measure student success," pressured state governments for reforms like national standards and is an example of a corporation that influences educational policies and funds research that pushes the demand for its products.

The deregulated charter-school movement is dominated by those who support it for its money-making potential, such as hedge fund directors and finance capitalists that control charters in most urban areas. The board of trustees of New York City's Harlem Children's Zone, for example, comprises CEOs of banks, corporations, and hedge funds, with no teachers, parents, or students. The millions of dollars Harlem Children's Zone invests in a hedge fund in turn make millions for that fund. While teachers in charter schools are typically paid less than in standard public schools, the top 25 hedge fund managers took in an average of $1 billion each in 2009, enough to pay for 658,000 entry-level teachers. Hedge fund managers are also involved in political lobbying groups like Democrats for Education Reform and Education Reform Now that spend millions of dollars to challenge state legislation that would limit the number of charter schools and to support efforts to abolish teacher tenure.

Venture philanthropy, as practiced by the Gates, Broad, and Walton foundations, for example, is another way donors decide what social transformation they want to engineer and then design and fund projects to implement their market-based goals for over-hauling public education—"choice," competition, deregulation, ac-countability, and data-driven decision making. In 2009, 43 percent of all urban superintendents were graduates of the Broad Founda-tion's training program for professionals in business, the military, and law. Secretary Duncan hired those coming from the staffs of the Gates and Broad foundations, and other advocacy groups and school management organizations that they fund, for top positions in the Department of Education. In 2010, the Gates and Broad foundations funded NBC News's *Education Nation*, which was heavily weighted in favor of the Duncan–foundation agenda. They also funded *Waiting for Superman*, widely critiqued as superficial and biased against public education.

Democratic reformers argue that officials who answer to the voters should run public schools; the Gates, Broad, and Walton foundations aren't accountable to anyone. Local educators, parents, and communities should be responsible for decisions about public schools, not corporate CEOs and hedge fund managers.

Alternative Voices

This book is not an argument for maintaining the status quo. We need better schools. But the media's attention given to market-driven approaches makes it nearly impossible for the public to recognize the value of public education as it currently exists in many schools and to envision the potential for effective innovation. In fact, while there is very little research or evidence to support the effectiveness of many federal initiatives, research and best practices show that other methods besides high-stakes testing can best achieve accountability.

Corporate-connected charter schools, high-stakes tests, merit pay, evaluating teachers by student test scores, firing teachers, and closing schools do not achieve success for a wide range of diverse students. Rather, adequate resources, professional development for teachers, smaller class sizes, and collaboration between schools and communities do. The contributors to this volume demonstrate this potential for public education.

The ambush of public education over the past thirty years is becoming an onslaught that is taking a heavy toll on students, educators, parents, and communities. In the face of these overwhelming, top-down agendas, people have not been silent, but have been speaking, acting, organizing, and resisting. These are the voices of the people you will hear in *Educational Courage: Resisting the Ambush of Public Education.*

Notes

1. Howard L. Fleischman, Paul J. Hopstock, Marisa P. Pelczar, and Brooke E. Shelley, "Highlights from PISA (2009): Performance of U.S. 15-Year-Old Students in Reading, Mathematics, and Science Literacy in an International Context," National Center for Education Statistics (December 2010), 15, nces.ed.gov/.
2. The Editors, "Goodbye to Schools as Businesses," *Rethinking Schools* 23, no. 1 (2009): 6.
3. Stan Karp, "NCLB's Selective Vision of Equality: Some Gaps Count More Than Others," in *City Kids: City Schools*, eds. William Ayers, Gloria Ladson-Billings, Gregory Michie, and Pedro Noguera (New York: New Press, 2008), 222–23.
4. Matthew Springer, "Teacher Pay for Performance," National Center on Performance Incentives, Vanderbilt University (2010).
5. Wayne Au, "Neither Fair Nor Accurate: Research-Based Reasons Why High-Stakes Tests Should Not Be Used to Evaluate Teachers," *Rethinking Schools* 25, no. 2 (2010/2011): 34–38.
6. Christine Sleeter, "Multicultural Education and NAME: Claiming the Future," keynote address, National Association for Multicultural Education Annual Conference, Las Vegas, 2010.

2. One Teacher's Cry

Susan J. Hobart

I'm a teacher. I've taught elementary school for eleven years. I've always told people, "I have the best job in the world." I crafted curricula that made students think, and they had fun while learning. At the end of the day, I felt energized. Today, more often than not, I feel demoralized.

While I still connect my lesson plans to students' lives and work to make it real, this no longer is my sole focus. Today I have a new nickname: testbuster. Singing to the tune of "Ghostbusters," I teach test-taking strategies similar to those taught in Stanley Kaplan prep courses for the SAT. I spend an inordinate amount of time showing students how to "bubble up," the term for darkening those little circles that accompany multiple-choice questions on standardized tests.

I am told the time we spend preparing for and administering the tests, analyzing the results, and engaging in professional development will help our children become proficient on this annual measure of success and will pay off by reducing the academic achievement gap between white children and children of color.

But what I know is that I'm not the teacher I used to be. And it takes a toll. Today, when I speak with former colleagues, they are amazed at the cynicism creeping into my voice.

What has changed?

High-stakes testing is certainly a big part of the problem. The children I test are from a wide variety of abilities and backgrounds. Whether they have a cognitive disability, speak entry-level English, or have speech or language delays, everyone takes the same test, and the results are posted. Special education students may have some accommodations, but they take the same test and are expected to perform at the same level as general education students. Students new to this country or with a native language other than English must also take the same test and are expected to perform at the same level as children whose native language is English. Picture yourself taking a five-day test in French after moving to Paris last year.

The No Child Left Behind Act is an example of a policy that is one-size-fits-all. But any experienced teacher knows how warped a yardstick that is.

As an educator, I know these tests are only one measure, one snapshot, of student achievement. Unfortunately, they are the make-or-break assessment that determines our status with the Department of Education.

They are the numbers that are published in the paper.

They are the scores that home buyers look at when deciding if they should move into a neighborhood.

They are the numbers that are pulled out and held over us, as more and greater rigidity enters the curriculum.

In an increasingly diverse public school setting, there is no one educational pedagogy that fits all students. We study and discuss differentiated curricula, modify teaching strategies, and set just-right reading levels to scaffold student learning. But No Child Left Behind doesn't care about that. It takes no note of where students started or how much they may have progressed.

As a teacher, I measure progress and achievement for my students on a daily basis. I set the bar high, expecting a lot.

I don't argue with the importance of assessment; it informs my instruction for each child.

I don't argue with the importance of accountability; I believe in it strongly—for myself and my students.

I have empathy for our administrators who have to stand up and be told that we are "challenged schools." And I have empathy for our administrators who have to turn around and drill it into our teacher heads, telling us we must do things "this" way to get results. I feel for them. They are judged on the numbers, as well.

No Child Left Behind, Race to the Top, and other federal and corporate education policies are symptoms of a larger problem: the attack on public education itself. Like the school-choice effort, which uses public funds to finance private schools and cherry-pick the best students, these policies are designed to punish public schools and to demonstrate that private is best.

But I don't think we've turned a corner that we can't come back from. Public education has been a dynamic vehicle in our country since its inception. We must grapple with maintaining this progressive institution. Policymakers and educators know that education holds out hope as *the* great equalizer in this country. It can inspire and propel a student, a family, a community.

The state where I teach has a large academic achievement gap for African Americans and low-income children. That is unacceptable. Spending time, money, and energy on testing everyone with a one-size-fits-all test will not eliminate or reduce that gap.

Instead, we need teacher-led professional development and more local control of school budgets and policymaking. Beyond that, we need to address the economic and social issues many children face, instead of punishing the schools that are trying to do right by these students.

We've got things backwards today. Children, not the testing companies, should be in the front seat. And teachers should be rewarded for teaching, not for being Stanley Kaplan tutors.

Ten years ago, I taught a student named Cayla. A couple of months ago, I got a note from her, one of those things that teachers thrive on. "Ms. Hobart was different than other teachers, in a good way," she wrote. "We didn't learn just from a textbook; we experienced the topics by 'jumping into the textbook.' We got to construct a rainforest in our classroom, have a fancy lunch on the Queen Elizabeth II, and go on a safari through Africa. What I learned ten years ago still sticks with me today. When I become a teacher, I hope to inspire my students as much as she inspired hers."

Last week, I received a call from Niecy, another student from that class ten years ago. She was calling from southern Illinois to tell me she was graduating from high school this month and had just found out that she has won a scholarship to a college in Indiana. I was ecstatic in my happiness for her. We laughed, and I told her I was looking at a photo of her on my wall; she is building a pyramid out of paper bricks with her classmates.

I also had a recent conversation with Manuel in a grocery parking lot. He reminded me of my promise eight years ago to attend his high school graduation. I plan to be there.

Cayla and Niecy and Manuel are three of the reasons I teach. They are the reasons that some days this still feels like a passion and not a job. They are the fires that fuel my passion. They are the lifeboats that help me ride this current wave in education.

Eight or ten years from now, I want former students to contact me and tell me a success story from their lives. I don't want to be remembered as the teacher who taught them how to sing "Testbusters" or to "bubble up." I want to be remembered as a teacher who inspired them to learn.

Susan Hobart is a National Board–certified teacher and recipient of the 2011 Elementary Educator of the Year from the University of Wisconsin.

3. Rachel's Plea

Wendy J. Goodman

She turned ten last week. This morning she wakes in an unfamiliar bed at a psychiatric hospital. She had a nervous breakdown. In fourth grade.

Bright. Always exploring. Once, she played wherever she went. Dressing up, laughing, and giggling with friends. Now she cries to be allowed to be a kid, play with friends and baby dolls. Child of the twenty-first century, there's pressure, demands, expectations she must face. Today she's evaluated by a psychiatrist. Severe depression.

Third grade. High-stakes test is coming, gathering momentum. The president, the governor, the school board say, "Raise test scores!" The principal hammers the teachers: "Raise test scores!" Test-taking practice. Standardized stomachaches during test week, sleepless nights. She ponders her future, "If I graduate from high school . . ." Alarmed parents respond, "What do you mean *if*?" "You know, the high school test. I'll never pass."

At school, she has a resource teacher who writes behavioral objectives that must be accomplished "with 80 percent accuracy" and tells her, "You're not doing it right." At home, she still falls asleep nightly to a bedtime story. Until last night when she slept in the hospital.

Fourth grade. This year. Homework replaces play. Family time competes with spelling, math worksheets, and practice for tests. She takes homework seriously: it consumes afternoon, evening. Parents say "bedtime," and she cries, "I'm not done." If homework's not done, teacher won't ever be pleased.

Test-taking practice. She must take it seriously. Testing is coming. Teacher said so. Momentum gathers. Too much classwork—no time for physical education or organized play—and test-taking practice. Don't leave any blank, eat number-two pencils, and bring hearty breakfasts.

She puts her head down. "I can't do it." Tears drip down her cheek. It's too big a mountain for one little girl. Her crying continues throughout the school day. Daddy arrives. She hugs him tight but doesn't stop crying. "Daddy, I'll die of another test week."

Evening she cries or laments her shortcomings, in painful sadness. Not brother's kind teasing or Daddy's bad jokes or talking with Mom provide any relief. She wants to know why she's feeling so bad and begs to be taken somewhere for help and insightfully declares, "It isn't my fault. It isn't my fault. But whose fault is it?"

Sadness engulfs her. Weeping continues. Sunlight locked out. They seek out a doctor. Their child is hurt. Hope lost to despair, she exchanges her street clothes for hospital garb. That night, in her empty bedroom, her parents ponder, whose fault is it?

Fourth-grade nervous breakdowns should never occur. She cries to be safe from test mania. Alone in the psych ward, she weeps.

Wendy Goodman, the mother of three children, holds an MA in reading from the University of Arizona and is currently a special-education preschool teacher.

Part II

Introduction: "I Won't Be a Part of This!"—Educators, Parents, Students, and Community Members Resist

It can be challenging to find the voices we need to speak out against injustice, and even harder when the injustices are deeply embedded in our lives and our jobs. Teachers struggle when they are employed by educational systems that they believe are harming the children they teach. Parents also wrestle with what actions to take to change their children's school experiences. Nonetheless, educators, parents, students, and concerned community members have found ways to speak out about the injustices they've experienced in spite of the consequences they may have faced.

Write What You Know

There are many ways to raise our voices. We can take pen to paper, or fingers to keyboard, and write about the travesties we observe with the hope of educating others, expanding their worldviews, raising consciousness, and changing policies. Sometimes we feel the pain of dehumanizing educational policies so deeply and perceive the damages so clearly that we feel we must say, "No! I won't be part of this!" The narratives in this section reflect the voices of people, like many thousands of others across the nation, who have found ways—as individuals or small groups—to say no.

Raising our voices through the written word is a way to say publicly, "I disagree, I resist." Those who write a letter to an official, publish a letter to the editor, or write an op-ed piece have found the courage to step out of their personal worlds and publicly write about their ideas and their actions.

This section includes the voices of people of all ages. The young adults candidly share their powerful feelings of desperation in hope that their words will encourage adults to change these hurtful policies. A high school student represented the feelings of many of his peers when he wrote, in a booklet of student voices, "I tried SO HARD to get good grades despite my disability and still could not receive a diploma. It was like dangling a carrot in front of a rabbit without ever intending to let him eat it. What a cruel joke."

In our sound-bite culture, people are not encouraged to think about the assumptions underlying current educational policy. But when we can expose these assumptions, others may reflect on them and gain new insights. For example, author and researcher Alfie Kohn encourages readers to think about the illogical assumptions underlying the National Standards Movement, an effort leading to national tests. He asks readers to consider whether a single group of people who frame the standards should determine what happens in every public school in the country and whether uniformity is the same thing as excellence or equity. To the extent that our words can encourage readers to reflect and think deeply and critically, they contribute to the thought necessary to resistance.

Individuals Say No

Armed with new insights and buttressed by different kinds of data, some of the authors in this section have taken action to say no within the contexts of their schools and communities. These include working within the system to say, "No! I won't take this test," or to advocate for their children to opt out of tests or practice small acts of disobedience. Others—after doing all they could to fight damaging policies—have ultimately said, "No, I won't be part of this," and resigned from a system they believe does harm.

Young people themselves have also courageously said no. Fourth-grader Macario Guajardo announced to his parents one morning, "I think I want to protest the TAKS [Texas Assessment of Knowledge and Skills]. . . . I don't like what it's doing to my school." Macario couldn't have anticipated the impact of his action, which, like some initially small resistances, resulted in a *New York Times* story and coverage in other national media outlets.

Others have felt compelled—in spite of their deep love for their students and their profession—to resign in order to maintain their integrity. Nate Walker narrates the story of his decision to resign from a Detroit corporate charter school because of its "no excuses, whatever it takes policies," data-driven overtesting, anti-union campaign, and policies that undermine civil rights.

Former Nebraska Commissioner of Education Doug Christensen and assessment expert Chris Gallagher write about the power of refusal and tell the story of Nebraska, the one state that said no to NCLB. Doug and Chris explain: "We felt that the dictates of NCLB violated and undermined what we knew to be good and right in terms of advancing teaching and learning. We knew there was a better way."

The bedrock principle for Doug and Chris was that teachers who spent their days with kids were the most important decision makers in education. Nebraska was committed to a system of assessment and accountability built on local initiative, where teachers were major players. Many times Doug had said, "There will not be a state test as long as I am commissioner." But in 2008, when the Nebraska legislature passed a law to comply with NCLB, thus giving the federal government the power to shape of curriculum and instruction, Doug and Chris kept their values intact by saying no and resigned.

Neha Singhal enthusiastically joined Teach For America (TFA) after college and looked forward to making a difference in the lives of students and to having an impact on change in the educational system. Once enrolled, however, she became very concerned about the way TFA ignored issues of poverty and institutional racism and trained corps members to focus only on achieving high test scores. She left TFA after three months. "I have since realized that I want to go about becoming a teacher the right way. I've entered a university-based master's program in social justice education to learn the tools and pedagogy to be effective for my students."

Saying No, Taking Leadership, Building Community

An individual's *no* can sometimes catalyze the creation of a broader community of resistance by educating others and garnering allies. Our creative rebellion can spark others' creativity. Our *no's* to the educational policy attacks on our communities, particularly on communities of color, can foster organizing efforts that engage more people in the struggle.

Latricia Wilson decided not to let Tennessee's high school exit exam deter her from her dream of entering college. Finding allies to help her bring a suit against the state, she called public attention to the unfairness of one test score keeping an otherwise successful high school student from graduating and pursuing higher education. Latricia's decision to challenge the system contributed to the legislature's elimination of the state test. She went on to attend college.

Neoliberal educational policies have targeted communities of color more than others. These policies have been used to attack ethnic studies and multicultural education and to impose rigid testing programs that set up English-language learners for failure. And they have been used to close neighborhood schools and replace them with charter schools with selective admission policies that keep out neighborhood children. Individuals in communities of color have stood up to these attacks and inspired others to do the same.

Curtis Acosta writes about the Raza Studies Program in the Tucson High Magnet School that, for ten years, said no to the prepackaged, test-driven curriculum and yes to a rigorous curriculum based on self-reflection, cultural studies, critical thought, and social justice. This was a program that, by encouraging an authentic exploration of Mexican American history and culture tied to state standards, closed the achievement gap between Latino/a and European American students. This program enabled all students to believe in their academic identity and to hope for the future. Acosta's, his colleagues', and students' leadership to save the program—despite state legislators' racially motivated efforts to control education—was driven by the desire to maintain a core program value: love. "What was at the center of our classes was a deep capacity to love one another. This is another area that the 'high-stakes' testing movement disregards."

For many educators nationwide, the capacity to create community and support young people in valuing themselves and each other is a central educational goal. Educators around the country who fight high-stakes testing are fighting for the power to maintain a caring community in their classrooms, and many, like Acosta, struggle to keep multicultural and social justice central to education.

Parents often decide that they "can't be part of this" when they come to understand how "de-form" policies are affecting their children. They can do this only when they reject an ideology that pervades the mainstream media and blames schools and teachers for not preparing students well enough for the tests. Many parents who have come to understand how the tests set up certain children for failure have become leaders in organizing parents to say no to high-stakes education nationwide.

If we hope to raise audacious children, we must be audacious ourselves. As the writers of the narratives in this section show, there are many ways to be audacious and say, "I won't be part of this!"

4.   Voices of Students with Disabilities

Kids As Self Advocates (KASA)

Kids As Self Advocates or KASA is a group that seeks to empower the voices of young people with disabilities on issues that affect them, including educational policy. As a youth-led project, KASA comprises several leadership bodies including a board that directs the project and a task force made up of younger youth. They work together on large-scale projects doing qualitative research such as surveying and obtaining questionnaires and personal accounts to bring disabled youths' voices to issues and illuminate their perspective. It is the children's perspective that is so valuable to education policy.

One recent project the task force took on was devoted to standardized testing and the new policy of exit exams at the high school level. KASA asked, How do these policies affect students with disabilities? It collected surveys as well as experiences of students with disabilities from around the country to find an answer and reported them in a publication, "Standardized Testing: What Youth with Disabilities Have to Say." The voices of these students follow.

Question: What are the problems with standardized testing?
[Standardized testing is] absolutely unfair!! In our state, it is keeping most youth with disabilities from getting a diploma. One problem is that they [administrators] don't really want kids with special needs taking the tests to begin with, because that will "mess up" the results for that particular teacher, school, system, etc. Also, the list of accommodations is so limited in our state that many students don't have adequate support to take the tests.—High school student from Alabama

The norms are not based on people with disabilities. Some questions on standardized tests even assume an able-body majority-based perspec-

tive. I think that this population [people with disabilities] needs to be considered not only while writing/compiling tests but also during the actions/consequences that follow [in response to the results]. Timed tests can especially be challenging for people with certain disabilities that can make the task of writing quickly a challenge. While accommodations may be available, they almost always rely on the student to take the initiative to ask for them. Students may not know these accommodations exist or they may be embarrassed to stop the test in the middle of the opening instructions.—High school student from Florida

I think they do a disservice to everyone, whether you have a disability or not because there is no real educating going on in the classroom; teaching is no longer an art. Teachers are told exactly how to present information and there is no time to go over things when pupils don't understand them. There is no more creativity in the classroom. It expects all students to fit into a cookie-cutter mold and doesn't take differences, including cultural differences, into account.—High school student from Louisiana

Question: How do standardized tests make you feel?
The standardized testing makes me feel like I am stupid and am not worth being a productive member of society. My mom tells me that even though I did not get my diploma that I deserved one because I did do a good job with finishing all twelve years of school. I know that it has caused great distress in my own life knowing that I tried SO HARD to get good grades in school despite my disability and still I could not receive a diploma. It was like dangling a carrot in front of a rabbit without ever intending to let him eat it. What a cruel joke.—High school student from Indiana

I feel like I have been left behind, even though my grades are good, I can't take tests. It isn't easy for my mom to go to the meetings anymore to try to get me help; they make her cry and tell her to take me out of the school. I don't want to leave the school—I want to be a senior in high school.—High school student from Texas

**Question: What do you want lawmakers to
know about standardized testing?**

*It does not work for everyone. That is like giving everyone the same blood
pressure pill for hypertension, or giving everyone the same amount of
insulin for every diabetic person. Sounds ludicrous when you look at
it from a medical standpoint, doesn't it? How can you expect to shove
every child into the same category and expect them all to do at least
average or better? It just doesn't work that way. . . . [It] took away my
chance to make some sort of a difference in my life and society as a
whole. I can't even get a decent paying job without a diploma or go back
to school [college] if I wanted to.*—High school student from Indiana

*I was specifically told that I could not have any kind of help, tutoring,
or someone to read the questions to me so that I would have a chance
to choose the correct answer. Instead, because I did not get the help I
needed for my "DISABILITY," I ultimately failed the ISTEP Testing
and was not able to receive a DIPLOMA even though I went through
all twelve grades and maintained a "B" average in the learning disabled
class.*—High school student from Indiana

---

*Kids As Self Advocates is a national project of Family Voices, Albuquerque, New Mexico. You can visit KASA on the web at www.fvkasa.org.
To read and download the full report, "Standardized Testing: What
Youth with Disabilities Have to Say," visit KASA's "What's New" page.*

5. Debunking the Case for National Standards

Alfie Kohn

I keep thinking it can't get much worse, and then it does. Throughout the 1990s, one state after another adopted prescriptive education standards enforced by frequent standardized testing, often of the high-stakes variety. A top-down, get-tough movement to impose accountability began to squeeze the life out of classrooms.

A decade ago, many of us thought we had hit bottom, until the floor gave way and we found ourselves in a basement we hadn't known existed. Now every state had to test every student every year in grades three through eight, judging them (and their schools) almost exclusively by test scores and hurting the schools that needed the most help. Ludicrously unrealistic proficiency targets suggested that the federal law responsible was intended to sabotage rather than improve public education.

Today, we survey the wreckage. Talented teachers have abandoned the profession after having been turned into glorified test-prep technicians. Low-income teenagers have been forced out of school by do-or-die graduation exams. Countless inventive learning activities have been eliminated in favor of prefabricated lessons pegged to state standards.

And now we're informed that what we really need . . . is to standardize this whole operation from coast to coast.

Have we lost our minds? Because we're certainly in the process of losing our children's minds. Let's be clear about this latest initiative, which is being spearheaded by politicians, corporate CEOs, and companies that produce standardized tests. First, what they're trying to sell us are national standards. They carefully point out that the effort isn't driven by the federal government. But if all, or nearly all, states end up adopting identical mandates, that distinction doesn't amount to much.

Second, these standards will inevitably be accompanied by a national standardized test. "Standards alone," warns Dane Linn of the National Governors' Association, a key player in this initiative, "will not drive teaching and learning"—meaning, of course, the specific type of teaching and learning that the authorities require. Even if we took the advice of the late Harold Howe II, a former U.S. commissioner of education, and made the standards "as vague as possible," a national test creates a de facto national curriculum, particularly if high stakes are attached.

Third, a relatively small group of experts—far from classrooms—will be designing standards, test questions, and curricula for the rest of us. Incredibly, the official website of the Common Core State Standards Initiative insists that these will be "based on evidence" rather than reflecting anyone's "individual beliefs about what is important." But evidence can tell us only whether a certain method is effective for reaching a certain objective—for example, how instruction aligned to this standard will affect a score on that test. The selection of the goal itself—what our children will be taught and tested on—unavoidably reflects values and beliefs. Should those of a single group of individuals determine what happens in every public school in the country?

Advocates of national standards say they want all (American) students to attain excellence, no matter where they happen to live. The problem is that excellence is being confused with entirely different attributes, such as uniformity, rigor, specificity, and victory. Let's consider each in turn.

Are all kids entitled to a great education? Of course. But that doesn't mean all kids should get the *same* education. High standards don't require common standards. Uniformity is not the same thing as excellence—or equity. (In fact, one-size-fits-all demands may offer the illusion of fairness, setting back the cause of genuine equity.) To recognize these simple truths is to watch the rationale for national standards collapse into a heap of intellectual rubble.

I know of no evidence showing that students in countries as diverse as ours with national standards or curricula engage in unusually deep thinking or are particularly excited about learning. Even standardized-test results, such as those of the Trends in International Mathematics and Science Study, provide no support. On eighth-grade math and science exams, eight of the ten top-scoring countries had centralized education systems, but so did nine of the ten lowest-scoring countries in math and eight of the ten lowest-scoring countries in science.

So if students don't benefit from uniformity, who does? Presumably, corporations that sell curriculum materials and tests will enjoy lower costs. And then there are the policymakers who confuse doing well with beating others. If you're determined to evaluate students or schools in *relative* terms, it helps if they're all doing the same thing. But why would we want to turn learning into a competitive sport?

It's not only that national standards are unnecessary, they're also based on the premise that "our teachers cannot be trusted to make decisions about which curriculum is best for their schools," as the University of Chicago's Zalman Usiskin put it. Moreover, uniformity doesn't just happen—and continue—on its own. Someone has to make everyone apply the same standards. What happens, then, to educators who disagree with some of them or with, say, the premise that teaching must be split into separate disciplines? What are the implications of accepting a system characterized by what Deborah Meier has called "centralized power over ideas"?

I've written elsewhere about another error: equating harder with better and making a fetish of "rigorous" demands or tests whose primary virtue (if it's a virtue at all) is that they're really difficult. Read just about any brief for national standards and you'll witness this confusion in full bloom. A key selling point is that we're "raising the bar," even though, as Voltaire reminded us, "that which is merely difficult gives no pleasure in the end." Nor does it enhance learning.

Then, too, there is a conflation of quality with specificity. If children—and communities—are different from one another, the only safe way to apply one standard to all of them is to operate at a high level of abstraction: "We will help all students to communicate effectively," for example. (Hence Harold Howe's enduring wisdom about the need to keep things vague.) The more specific the standard, the more problematic to impose it on everyone. Pretty soon you're gratuitously defining some children as failures, particularly if standards are broken down by grade level.

The reasonable-sounding adjectives employed to defend an agenda of specificity—"focused," "coherent," "precise," "clear"— ought to make us nervous. If standards comprise narrowly defined facts and skills, then education consists of transmitting vast quantities of material to students, material that even the most successful may not remember, care about, or be able to use.

This is exactly what most state standards have already become, and it's where national standards are heading (even if, in theory, they could be otherwise). Specificity is what business groups and newspaper editorialists want. It's demanded by theorists who think being well educated mostly means knowing lots of facts. It's been a major criterion by which *Education Week* and conservative think tanks like the Thomas B. Fordham Institute evaluate standards documents. In any case, the politicians and corporate-sponsored groups pushing for these standards (Achieve, Inc., and the state governors) probably won't need much convincing; they'll give us specific in spades.

Finally, what's the *purpose* of demanding that every kid in every school in every state must be able to do the same thing in the same year, with teachers pressured to "align" their instruction to a master curriculum and a standardized test?

I once imagined a drinking game in which a few of those education reform papers from corporate groups and politicians were read aloud: You take a shot every time you hear "rigorous," "measurable," "accountable," "competitive," "world-class," "high(er) expectations," or "raising the bar." Within a few minutes, everyone would be so inebriated that they'd no longer be able to recall a time when discussions about schooling weren't studded with these macho managerial buzzwords.

But not all jargon is meaningless. This language has very real implications for what classrooms will look like and what education is (and isn't) all about. The goal here isn't to nourish children's curiosity, to help them fall in love with reading, to promote both the ability and the disposition to think critically, or to support a democratic society. Rather, a prescription for uniform, specific, rigorous standards is made to order for those whose chief concern is to pump up the American economy and triumph over people who live in other countries.

If you read the FAQs page on the Common Core State Standards website, don't bother looking for words like "exploration," "intrinsic motivation," "developmentally appropriate," or "democracy." Instead, the very first sentence contains the phrase "success in the global economy," followed immediately by "America's competitive edge."

If these standards are more economic than educational in their inspiration, more about winning than learning, devoted more to serving the interests of business than to meeting the needs of kids, then we've merely painted a twenty-first-century facade on a hoary, dreary model of school-as-employee-training. Anyone who recoils from that vision should strenuously resist a proposal for national standards that embodies it.

Yes, we want excellent teaching and learning for all, although our emphasis should be less on *achievement* (read: test scores) than on students' *achievements.* Offered a list of standards, we should scrutinize each one, but also ask who came up with them and for what purpose. Is there room for discussion and disagreement—and not just by experts—regarding what, and how, we're teaching and how authentic our criteria are for judging success? Or is this a matter of "obey or else," with tests to enforce compliance?

The standards movement, sad to say, morphed long ago into a push for standardization. The last thing we need is more of the same.

Alfie Kohn (www.alfiekohn.org) is the author of twelve books on education and human behavior.

6.   Resisting the State Test: The Story of an Eleven-Year-Old, *Niño Rebelde*

Francisco Guajardo

In February 2005, my son Macario refused to take the Texas school test, the TAKS; he was in the fifth grade. The Texas Assessment of Knowledge and Skills, or TAKS, is administered to public school students in the state and is the cornerstone of its accountability system. During the past generation, the TAKS has become the centerpiece of the school reform movement, and it has wreaked havoc on communities, schools, families, and countless children. My son responded to this havoc by refusing to take the test. His act of resistance catapulted him into the national spotlight, but it also challenged the education establishment in south Texas, and beyond, to pay closer attention to the increasing plight of children as they face conditions of undue stress in public schools.

The story really began in January 2004 when Macario developed a facial tic, an involuntary and incessant head jerk that he could not control. The head bobbing convinced my wife and me to take him to the family doctor. Upon examination, the doctor said Macario appeared fine, though he did seem a bit stressed. "What's going on at home?" the doctor asked.

"Things are normal at home," I said. "What about school? How are things there?" the doctor asked. Before I responded, Macario pronounced, "It's the TAKS! There's a lot of pressure at school to pass the TAKS!"

The doctor stated he had seen a number of other children who had come in because of stress symptoms, and he added that both children and parents admitted the source of the stress was the TAKS.

The doctor had no good answer for how to address Macario's stress, nor did he prescribe any medication. He only offered a blunt criticism: "This testing business in the schools is crazy, and it's counterproductive."

About this same time, I received an invitation to deliver the opening address at a national conference of educators. During that school year, No Child Left Behind (NCLB) was quickly descending upon the entire country, and because I was a Texas educator, conference organizers believed I could bring some Texas insight to the conference. The Texas brand of school reform, after all, was the blueprint upon which NCLB was based, and conference organizers were curious to hear about the effectiveness of Texas's school reform from the mouth of a Texas educator.

As I thought about my presentation, Macario was foremost on my mind, so I asked him for an interview. I explained my purpose and the nature of the conference, and told him that his voice would be more important than anything I could say about the school reform movement in Texas. He agreed to do it, so we drove to his elementary school, which we used as the backdrop for a video interview. I asked him to reflect on his experiences at school and to share some thoughts on the TAKS. I pinned a wireless microphone to his jacket and turned on the video camera. His comments were poignant and very revealing. I took the raw footage, edited a short video, and took Macario's voice with me to the North Dakota Study Group (NDSG) conference in Chicago.

The video was a big hit at the NDSG conference and sparked lively conversation. I received a number of requests for copies of Macario's interview, and subsequently sent copies to about a dozen people across the country. In California, educators used it as an organizing tool, as they held community meetings with parents who angrily contemplated how best to respond to the test-heavy NCLB policies. New York City educators used the video for similar purposes, though one creative elementary teacher showed the video to her third-grade students and asked them to write letters to Macario.

A packet from the Muscota New School arrived in my mailbox with those letters.

One child wrote, "Dear Macario, we are proud of you for speaking up against the test." Another said, "Dear Macario, did you have a hard time on the test cause sometimes I have a hard on it. Do you get it wrong or right? Do you hate test I hate it too."

And another said: "Dear Macario, I feel sorry for you that you have a test every week. But your [*sic*] not the only one, in my old school everyday [*sic*] we have a test."

Even the teacher, Louisa Cruz-Acosta, sent a letter. "I think you did a wonderful thing by making that video," she said. "My students would love to meet you." Additionally, Louisa sent Macario a copy of *Narrative of the Life of Frederick Douglass, an American Slave.* Macario was already familiar with the story of Douglass, but the fact he received the book as a gift spurred new family conversations and, perhaps most importantly, gave Macario ideas about how one historical figure demonstrated acts of great courage during a time of deep personal and social distress.

The book and the letters transformed Macario. He gained a new realization of the power of his words and the power of his story, and he began to imagine that he could be even more courageous than simply voicing his views on video. Privately, he began to think about protesting the TAKS.

When the fourth-grade year ended, his facial tic went away within days, as he began to enjoy a summer of endless play and family time. But then fall arrived, and with it returned the stressful conditions of school. Within two weeks of the new school year, he became irritable and frustrated, and the facial tic returned. I picked him up from school one afternoon and noticed he was especially contemplative.

We arrived at our home, he said, "Daddy, sit down, I want to talk to you." Sit down? This must be important, I thought, because he rarely said that to me. He sounded very serious.

He then said, "I think I want to protest the TAKS test. I don't want to take it. I don't know how I would do that, but I don't want to take the TAKS." I asked him, "What do you mean you want to protest the TAKS? Do you know what that means? Do you know what you're saying?"

He responded, "No, not really. All I know is that I don't like the test and don't want to take it. I don't know how I would protest it, but I was thinking that I just wouldn't go to school on the day of the test. I think I need your help on this, Daddy."

I liked what I heard, because I had seen the pressure build in him and had seen him get physically sick from the anxiety of the test. As an educator myself, I understood the insanity of the testing culture in the public schools.

But there was a bigger family issue at work here, because my wife is also a teacher in the same school district where Macario was planning to protest.

I asked him, "You know your mother is a teacher in the district? And you know that this could be a really huge deal? But tell me, what's the real reason? Why do you really want to do this?"

"All I know," he said, "is that I don't like what the test does to my school. They've cut recess, they cut a lot of things that kids like to do, the fun stuff, and all they do is force us to study for the test. I just don't like what this test does to my school." With those words, Macario convinced me that I had to support him, and that I had to convince my wife to support him.

When my wife came home from school, I told her about Macario's plan. She reacted with great emotion. "Did you put him up to this?" she asked me. "No," I said. "It's entirely his idea."

My wife wasn't convinced, so she decided to question Macario. They sat together for just a few minutes, when Macario said to her, "Mommy, I don't like what the test does to my school." That's all she needed to hear. The words were simple, pure, and powerful. And that day Macario stopped bobbing his head. The facial tic would be gone forever.

From that day forward, Macario and I developed a strategy. We had several months before the administration of the TAKS the following February. We decided that first he would tell his classmates that he was about to protest the unfairness of the test. He was firm in his belief and wanted to take a stand. He made it clear to them that this was not an impulsive decision, nor was it a frivolous act. His classmates responded positively, and some even said they'd join him on a protest march to the state capital.

Next, he talked to his teachers, and it turned out they were equally anxious to engage him in that conversation. One teacher even asked him to address the entire class, an experience he described with great enthusiasm. Next, we both explained his position to the school principal. Curiously, the principal told Macario she was proud of him for following his conviction, though she hoped he would still take the test.

During the second month of explanations, I visited both the assistant superintendent in charge of instruction and the superintendent. I explained that Macario's planned resistance was his honest way of saying that he'd had enough of the abusive test-prepping practices at his elementary school. I told them I was in complete support of Macario's position and suggested to them they should follow Macario's lead by keeping every child in the school district from taking the state-mandated test.

The school district administrators did not disagree with Macario's position; they actually told me they admired him, and believed his act of resistance was justified. They even felt compelled to share horrific stories about a number of children who were devastated by the intense pressure of the test.

"On the day of the test, Mr. Guajardo," said the assistant superintendent, "one child will bring her rosary to school, and she will rub the cross to the point where her hands will bleed. She's done that over the years, consistently on test days." "We have another child," said the superintendent, "who pulls her hair out, literally, because the pressure is too much on her."

Both senior administrators continued with the stories in a surreal display of good-hearted school leaders allowing horrific conditions to exist in their schools. I was heartbroken as I listened to the stories.

I asked the superintendent, "You allow this to happen?" "There's nothing I can do," he said. "It's the law." "Sir," I said to him, "you would be a national hero if you demand that this madness stop. You would be a hero to people across the country if you simply decided no child in your school district would be subjected to such experiences!" "I wish I could," he said.

But he couldn't, of course, because in his mind, his employment depended on his ability to lead a school district toward good test results, even if the policies that dictate high-stakes testing engendered an oppressive school climate. "I agree with Macario," said the superintendent, "but my hands are tied."

The following week, Macario protested the state test. He spent the day of the test with his grandmother. They prepared several *salsas* of *chile,* had a good conversation, and posed for pictures for a *New York Times* reporter sent to south Texas to capture images of a child the *Times* called "a school exam's conscientious objector." Another news medium called him "*el niño rebelde*" (the rebel child).

Macario had not intended to be a *niño rebelde;* he had simply acted on his own sense of right and wrong, the way an honest eleven-year-old would, innocently, and without pretense. To Macario, Robert E. Lee Elementary was a test factory, and he believed the high-stakes testing environment created a type of school environment that was not good for him and not good for other kids either. His act of protest was an act of honest courage.

Days after the test, and after a time of frenzied media attention, Macario and I reflected on the meaning of his protest. He was proud of himself for acting on his own conviction and appreciated the positive reinforcement he received from family, friends, and even others in the school. He also expressed deep disappointment with the outcome, regretting he was the only student from his school, or from the entire south Texas region, to wage such a protest.

But Macario also saw how his act of resistance changed the behaviors of teachers and principals in his school. He had had an impact on how teachers taught, how principals led, and how the school district leadership thought about its TAKS preparation approach. Countless stories from teachers and school leaders described how they altered their practices because of Macario's protest. In short, Macario's story is one of courage and possibility; it's one of an eleven-year-old child whose act of resistance forced a school and a community to change.

Francisco Guajardo is professor of educational leadership at the University of Texas Pan American and the proud father of Macario.

7. There Is No Rubric for Imagination: Organizing against a Charter School Gone Corporate

Nate Walker

As a public school teacher, I was always skeptical about the role of charter schools run by private companies with public dollars. But in 2008, when I became a casualty of massive layoffs in the Detroit Public Schools, I learned firsthand what can happen when a charter school imposes an "efficiency and accountability model" on our educational system that glosses over the real and complex issues of children and education.

University Preparatory Academy (UPA) burst into Detroit's educational world in 2000 and quickly gained favor with progressive educators as an example of everything the charter school movement was supposed to promise: innovation, decentralized decision making, student-centered education, and community partnerships. In fact, UPA had gained so much momentum in the charter landscape that what began as a middle school became its own district, complete with two elementary schools and a high school. Its founder acknowledged that educational inequity was the result of an antiquated "factory approach to schooling" and kicked around words like "radical change." The early UPA was a place where teachers were advisers, clusters of classrooms were called houses, and the school community made decisions together.

At the time, I was working in one of those big factory schools— a nine-hundred-student middle school where teachers were called teachers and many of them wore years of frustration and exhaustion on their faces. By contrast, the UPA advisers were proud to work at their school; they trumpeted the school's small classes, project-based learning, and "whole child" values. They also talked about the freedom to be innovative and to do "real things" with their students.

While I envied the support my colleagues received for project-based learning and their role in a school community committed to education as a practice of social justice, I wasn't ready to leave Room 106 at Cerveny Middle School on Detroit's West Side. I had learned that if I appeased the administrators when it came to the things they cared about most—managing my students and keeping others out of the hallway during passing time—I could teach in a way that was similar to what I had perceived was happening at UPA. Plus, there was something about Cerveny that I couldn't shake. In many ways, it was not the school that kept me, but the neighborhood and the families I had gotten to know over the years. But, while I loved Cerveny, the brick walls couldn't keep many of the challenges of the neighborhood from interrupting a school day.

UPA was a destination for devoted teachers who were lured by its "innovative" approach; they became some of my closest friends. We would share lesson ideas and talk shop. When my students performed a play that they wrote at Cerveny, UPA advisers showed up, and when their students put together a film on issues of food justice, I went to the screening.

UPA was growing and expanding, and after being laid off at Cerveny because of budget cuts, I followed my colleagues there. At first, I was surprised at how much like Cerveny it actually was. Before the academic year started, we received professional development for our new math curriculum—the same curriculum used by the Detroit Public Schools. I was also told that our day would follow block scheduling. I was surprised to find that a school that had built its identity on being "progressive" was now adopting many of the practices of the system it outwardly criticized. Next I learned it was standardizing lessons, standardizing student goals, and standardizing a singular vision of student success: one defined by students' performance on standardized tests.

During these changes, the school founder adopted the "no excuses, whatever it takes" pump-up lingo that has become synonymous with so many charter schools. This language distracts listeners from the fact that they are working with children—living and breathing people—and instead loses teachers in a sea of phrases like "student growth" and "smart numbers." Policies that matched this language started to flood the school; the principal who had hired me resigned, uncomfortable delivering what would become known as "UPA 2.0," a program that would deliver the data, show measurable gains, and become the champion of urban education by conquering tests.

Right around the time our principal left, I became the seventh-grade lead adviser, which not only provided me with a bird's-eye view of a school trying to force a culture of achievement, but also gave me the responsibility of enforcing that culture's emphasis on data-driven instruction. In the past, UPA had recognized tests as one piece of an assessment picture, and its emphasis on other tools, like portfolios and exhibitions, was its strength. Now bubble sheets and computer programs began choking out these outcome measures. As assessment methods changed, so did learning experiences and school culture.

UPA now promoted the idea that educational reform effectively meant developing a more efficient factory, with more seat time, an extended school day, and higher student test scores incentivized by a merit-pay system. UPA 2.0 prided itself on its model for raising student achievement, a number that operates much like a bottom line. But it's a model that glosses over the needs of people, without trying to understand or address the root causes of many of the problems in urban communities. It doesn't acknowledge that the youth in these communities have the intellect and creativity to participate in solving those problems through educational experiences created for this purpose.

One March afternoon, when UPA announced it would be turning its "relentless commitment" up a notch, I remember experiencing a feeling I sometimes had at Cerveny—how the culture of the school, from the metal detectors to the discipline policies, made the school feel like a prison. And how, accordingly, sometimes the students acted like prisoners . . . and sometimes I acted like a prison guard. I was now afraid that the culture of producing student achievement at all costs would force me to see people as data points that I should move up a regression line or, in the worst of cases, remove from the sample. I hated that feeling.

I was afraid that our classroom would lose everything that I thought had made it a special place for adolescent writers discovering their own identities, thoughts, and voices. Standardized questions call for standardized answers, but, fortunately, adolescents are just starting to realize that the world is not such a standardized place. I liked to believe my classroom was a place where they could become themselves through their expositions. Creativity and curiosity cannot be neatly shaded in with a number-two pencil. I wondered how I would handle the pressure of our new culture? Would my students feel it in my voice? Would I ask them to play it safe as young writers? Would I use a rubric to score their imagination?

I was also concerned about my own willingness to take risks. Even in my first year at UPA, my classroom had gained the reputation as a refuge for students who were struggling academically or emotionally. My advisory absorbed many of the seventh grades' most challenging students. I enjoyed working with these students and they had an affinity for me. When the founder announced UPA's new plans, I thought of the students I had picked up along the way, the ones who were moved to my classroom. Some of them struggled academically, some were too distracted by the reality of their lives, and others wondered why they should care about school. Either way, they all ended up in my classroom where we would learn, laugh, and struggle together. Then I thought about myself. Next year, when I would be evaluated primarily on how my students tested, would I be penalized for welcoming struggling students into my room? Would I continue to make decisions based on the needs of students or would I succumb to the pressure to "be effective," and avoid helping certain students work through challenges? These questions were exhausting, but I decided that it was my responsibility as a teacher to raise them and to advocate for a type of education that respects children and challenges them to contribute to our world.

I knew many of UPA's new policies were not substantiated by

educational research. I knew that many administrators and policy-makers accept research studies like grocery shoppers pick canta-loupes, carefully choosing from a vast selection one that seems like a good fit at the time. Simply presenting a case against new UPA 2.0 policies would likely be a toothless endeavor. I knew that speaking out would peg me as not buying into UPA 2.0, which would be spun as opposing high expectations, not closing the achievement gap, and failing to believe in Detroit's youth. I also knew it would likely cost me my job.

Many of my colleagues shared my frustration that the impending changes at UPA were unnecessary and feared that the positive cul-ture that had been built during the first years of the school would be lost. A group of us formed the University Preparatory Academy Fed-eration of Teachers organizing committee with a simple demand: in-clude us in decisions that affect our students and our school. Within the first week of our campaign, 90 percent of the middle school staff signed membership cards. During that week, the school felt differ-ent. You could see it in the way staff members walked down the hall-way, as if, for the first time, their strides said, "this is our school too."

The news of our campaign eventually made its way to the admin-istration, which immediately scrambled to oppose our organizing efforts. The administrators held meetings to caution against union-ization and built a case against our cause, claiming *we* would destroy the school and the "familylike" atmosphere that the *administrators* created. They sternly asserted that forming a union would harm our students, who were from Detroit and needed "the best education."

When UPA's founder delivered this case at the middle school, the staff listened quietly and waited for the meeting to end. When it did, the founder pulled me aside and offered me a principal position at a school he was opening the following year. I politely declined.

The founder personally visited all the advisers at the middle school with the message that they were "a family" and all a union would do was "disrupt this atmosphere." He also doled out misin-formation, intimidated certain staff members, stroked the egos of others, and said that he finally "began to hear our voices." He then set up a district council where teachers elected representatives to help make decisions, as a way to undercut our union. Teachers at UPA, and every other charter school in Detroit, are at-will employees who can be fired at any time for any reason without due process. If teachers make a professional decision that the administration disagrees with, they can be terminated. Many advisers were afraid they would lose their jobs, and even though most supported our efforts, some were just too trusting of the founder and wanted to give the district council a chance. A combination of fear and guilt killed the drive.

Although we managed to slow several of the changes at UPA, the district council only gave the facade of collaborative decision making; it worked as long as it echoed the administration and concerned itself with helping to implement policies that narrowed the curriculum, drastically limited project-based learning, and emphasized standardized test preparation over all else.

At the end of the year, I informed UPA of my intentions to leave in a simple letter of resignation. I felt it was essential to discuss how Detroit and its children deserved more from education and needed voices willing to question what is now broad, sweeping reform. I did not want to fear for my job during these discussions.

Later, I encountered our school's superintendent. Before asking me about my decision, she gave me a puzzled look, one of fatigue and confusion, as if she wanted to say, "You caused all this mess, got a district council, and now you're leaving." Instead she just said, "Why?" I remember not knowing where to begin.

I wanted to tell her that I thought the changes at UPA represented everything that was wrong with what has become known as "educational reform," which cares more about student achievement than about students. I wanted to tell her this reform model was a narrow version of education that damaged people and communities. I wanted to tell her that every time they justified their policies by claiming it was in the name of civil rights, they diminished the causes of that movement. Martin Luther King Jr. once said, "When machines, computers, profit motives and property rights are considered more important than people . . . the giant triplets of racism, materialism, and militarism are incapable of being conquered." Finally, I wanted to tell her that we cannot expect communities to be better places unless we prepare our children to participate in them, as more than just college graduates or employees or consumers, and that unless we make it our business to educate to this end, what we are doing should not be called education.

In the end, I did not say much, except that I had too high an expectation for my students as people to view them as bubbles on a Scantron. I said that by questioning high-stakes testing, merit pay, and rote instruction, I was not lowering expectations, making excuses, or shrugging responsibility, and that I left because I was more concerned with education than the business of education.

Those pushing corporate educational "reform" will continue to praise UPA's corporate style. The administrators will continue to bask in the public relations spotlight, because that seems to be what is most important to them. Along the way, though, they will lose passionate educators and concerned families, who recognize that the business of education is not about building a brand around policy agenda; it is about nurturing people. This may not grab headlines or a spot on *Good Morning America*. But integrity, respect, and a commitment to people are not data-driven decisions and do not need marketing strategies. They are essential educational values.

Nate Walker lives in Detroit, where he is an organizer and educator.

8.   "No": The Power of Refusal

Doug Christensen and Chris W. Gallagher

Saying no, whether it's a simple refusal, a choice to take the high road, or a bold stand against injustice, is one thing. It's quite another to live with the consequences. Regardless of the reasons for saying no, you may end up leading a parade or watching from the sidelines. You may become a champion or a chump, a hero or a villain. You may win friends and admirers, or become marginalized and vilified by others, including colleagues and friends.

This is a story about saying no. This is a story about educators who, acting as leaders, find themselves in a situation where saying no is a personal and professional imperative. And this is our story: a tale of an unlikely but powerful partnership between a state commissioner of education (Doug) and a professor of English (Chris). Though this story centers on Nebraska's refusal to go along with the mandates of the No Child Left Behind Act, it is not about NCLB. It is about what happens when educators as leaders are called to stand against, to stand up, and to stand for what they believe. It is about the power and the consequences of refusal.

A Road Less Traveled

The 2001 No Child Left Behind Act was a wake-up call of sorts. It was intended to be a not so subtle reminder to states and schools that they weren't getting the job done and certainly were leaving too many kids behind. However, what it turned out to be was a wake-up call: the federal government was going to play a large, more intrusive, and more punitive role in state education agencies and local schools. With the law, the federal government bypassed states' authority over education, trampled the prerogatives of local school districts, and took professional decision making away from teachers. Many state leaders knew it, but they voiced their concerns only in private. Many teachers knew it, but their pleas were not heard.

Meanwhile, with their eyes on their pocketbooks, and in some cases with relief for the cover NCLB provided to their own top-down agendas, state leaders rushed to comply with this punitive high-stakes testing law. They created a race to see who could get there first and who would have the hand of the federal department of education placed on their heads in recognition of being a state that "gets it done."

But one state refused to jump on the bandwagon. Instead of marching in the reform parade, surely the easier choice, Nebraska chose to form its own parade down a road less traveled. This was not a cavalier decision; it did not result from a desire to be a maverick. Nebraska chose this road, knowing it would be ridiculed, would be marginalized as not "getting it," and would be put under enormous pressure, for a single, simple reason: we as Nebraskans thought what we wanted to do was simply the right thing to do. We felt that the dictates of NCLB violated and undermined what we knew to be good and right in terms of advancing teaching and learning in schools. We knew there was a better way.

That better way, that road less traveled, led us to the School-based, Teacher-led Assessment and Reporting System (STARS). The system was premised on the notion that the most important educational decisions happen in the classroom. And the system was premised on the notion that the best place from which to judge student performance, that is, student learning, was under the eyes of the professional teacher in the classroom. Who better to judge what students know and are able to do than the teachers who spend hours each day and days each year working directly with their students? No state-mandated and -centralized, standardized test could provide the same degree of quality in terms of judging what students have learned and how well they have learned.

Under STARS, teachers created assessments that emerged from the curriculum that was taught in the classroom. Districts and schools implemented their own assessment processes, which were evaluated for technical quality, starting with alignment to locally adopted standards. While most every state claimed coverage of all their standards by the state test, none actually found it possible. Under STARS, every standard found a place in the curriculum plans, and assessments covered the curriculum. In short, Nebraska built a statewide system of local assessments in which teachers, like other professionals, were in charge of the metrics of success (student learning) and the metrics of good practice (teaching).

For Nebraskans, as for Robert Frost's speaker in his famous poem, choosing the road less traveled made "all the difference." We learned a great deal on the road less traveled, especially about the power of refusal.

What We Learned on the Road Less Traveled

Saying No Can Buy Time

NCLB did not turn out to be a wake-up call for states in terms of achievement gaps, because the time lines for compliance were so short that people were busy scrambling to meet logistical deadlines and had little time or energy to deliberate over issues like "right" practice and other options than those dictated in the mandates. Serious conversations about values, principles, and purposes were crowded out. Few were asking, "Why are we doing this?"

By refusing to rush to comply with NCLB, Nebraskans bought time to get priorities straight. Instead of getting caught up in the problem-solving strategies of compliance or searching for market solutions to assessment and accountability, we stepped back to think hard about what we wanted for our kids, teachers, families, and communities. Instead of being seduced into the heady political game of status chasing and becoming a "player" in the federal government's eyes, Nebraskans developed a core set of values to serve as a framework for responding to any external mandate, including NCLB. We were able to explore and articulate these ideas because when we said no, we put ourselves in the eye of the storm. In the eye, we had actually created for ourselves some time and space (and calm) to think and act.

Systemic Coherence Emerges Only
from Fidelity to Core Principles

In truth, Nebraskans had been working on assessment and account-ability based on our own values, beliefs, and principles long before NCLB, and we continued to do so once it was enacted. We wanted standards that local schools adapted; local initiative and leadership as the driver of policy; diverse assessments that actually helped teach-ers teach and students learn; teachers at the lead of any reform effort designed to change classrooms and the work that went on in them; and above all, student learning at the center of everything we did. We weighed every decision made regarding STARS—including poten-tial changes based on the expectations of the federal government—carefully in light of these core principles. These core values, beliefs, and principles lent STARS a level of rationality and coherence that is exceedingly rare in the usually disjointed world of educational sys-tems. Certainly we could not have achieved this kind of coherence from cobbling together compliance activities.

Everyone Can March

STARS gained coherence from its adherents. While teachers and stu-dents were always at the center of STARS, everyone had a role to play. The policymakers—state board members, state and U.S. sena-tors, Nebraska Department of Education leaders—created envi-ronments conducive to teaching and learning. The professional developers supported teachers' assessment literacy to the district. Building administrators became leaders of learning communities. Parents and community members supported and participated in their schools' improvement. This statewide community of brave and brilliant advocates helped STARS succeed for nearly a decade in the midst of a federal policy environment that could not have been less supportive of its core principles.

We—Doug and Chris—marched, too, each in our own way. Of all the relationships that formed in our parade, perhaps none was stranger than the one between the two of us. We came from different places: one a Midwesterner through and through, the other a born-and-bred Northeasterner. We came from different perspectives: one the commissioner of education, the other a professor of English. And we had different styles: one outgoing and decisive, and the other quiet and more deliberate. Besides, while Doug was the public face of STARS, Chris was not—and never would be—entirely sold on all aspects of the system, though he admired Nebraska's attempt to design an alternative to the bandwagon state tests he'd seen elsewhere. In the years to come, Chris, as lead evaluator of the system, would both criticize and praise STARS. But our professional and personal friendships would remain, held together by the strength of our commitment to kids and their teachers. That friendship continues today. On our march down the road less traveled, we learned that sometimes the person you most want to march side-by-side with is not a like-minded ally, but a critical friend.

One critical-friend moment came in 1999, as STARS was just getting off the ground, and Chris published an article in which he wrote: "We are at present blessed with some measure of chaos. . . . [N]o one fully understands how assessment will play out in our state over the next several years."[1] Doug wondered: was Chris questioning his vision, or his resolve, or the extent to which Nebraskans would stand by STARS as it evolved? But as he reflected on Chris's words—*blessed* with chaos?—Doug began to think about chaos as a positive force for change, an opportunity to lead, not a problem to overcome. He thought of the old adage that "a captain never goes to the bridge when the weather is calm," and he knew he needed to have a steady hand as he worked with others to navigate the treacherous political waters ahead. He came to see that chaos, when confronted with courage and trusted colleagues, can lead to clarity and focus.

Sometimes, Politics Trumps Results

What Nebraskans built out of chaos *worked*. We know this because under Doug's leadership, the Nebraska Department of Education (NDE) implemented several processes for gathering data on the implementation and outcomes of STARS. Chris led a university-based evaluation team that conducted annual visits to the schools to see how STARS was working and check on the status of the implementation. The NDE also had a university professor consult and facilitate work groups and convene, host, and moderate the state's annual leadership-for-assessment conference. In addition, the NDE contracted research teams to do two independent studies to judge the validity and reliability of the STARS process.

In addition to significant and steady improvement in student achievement—the most important finding—the studies found strong technical quality of assessments used to measure students' learning, a shift toward data-informed instruction, significant growth in teachers' assessment literacy, teachers' increased ownership of STARS and their local assessment processes, increasing teacher leadership, and the development of collaborative learning cultures in schools.

Despite the voluminous and unchallenged documentation of STARS' successes, however, state legislators chose in 2008 to accept the U.S. Department of Education's interpretation that the only way to meet the requirements of NCLB was to implement a raft of state tests. This is not the place to recount the sad tale of the demise of STARS, but what we learned was that political machinations and political power trips can sometimes trump good educational practice. Indeed, at the public hearings, no one claimed that STARS wasn't working; the worry was that STARS was too different, too out of step with the national reform parade. If we had it to do all over again, we would not change much about STARS. But we would not assume that if the system worked, key state legislators would join our parade. And we would not underestimate how power struggles can undermine sound thought and conclusive data. We underestimated the pressure on officials (or their will to resist the pressure) to take the road *more* traveled by joining the NCLB bandwagon.

Sometimes Saying No Means Saying Goodbye

Values are great to have—until you have to live by them. For us, it was time to move on. We both made the painful personal decision to say no to Nebraska's new approach to standards and accountability.

Many times, Doug had said, "There will not be a state test as long as I am commissioner." He could not abandon his core values even though it would have been politically expedient to do so. Now was not the time to back off or back down from deep personal and professional values. On his last day at work, Doug stepped onto the elevator at 5:30 and pushed the button for the bottom floor. The next day, he would no longer be commissioner. He felt an emptiness and a nostalgia for his life as commissioner that he had loved and professional life from which he was walking away. But almost simultaneously, he felt another, more surprising emotion: gratitude. Fourteen years as chief state school officer: what a gift! Who gets to influence so many teachers, so many students, so many communities?

At a "celebration" lunch the next day, Doug's wife helped him understand something else. He confessed to her that he could not help but feel he had been "let go," even though he knew this was not really true. The saga had not ended the way he had hoped; he had lost. But she quickly corrected him: "You won the important battle. You walked away with your values intact. That is huge, and I'm proud of you for that." This is perhaps the best reason, and the best reward, for courage.

For Chris, the decision was much the same. Though he continued to quibble with some aspects of STARS, he had seen with his own eyes the positive difference it was making in the lives of kids, teachers, families, and communities. He had also seen the negative effects of high-stakes tests in other states, and he was not interested in working for or with that kind of system.

For the last time, Chris addressed Nebraska educators at the annual leadership for assessment conference just a few short months after the passage of the testing law. In his keynote address, he thanked the teachers and school administrators:

> You welcomed me into your schools, into your classrooms, and into your lives. . . . You offered me your time, your insights, and often some not-so-terrible cafeteria food. Though I was a virtual stranger to you, you showed me your cur-

riculum, your instruction, your assessment—the CIA. You taught me a new language full of words and acronyms once foreign: CRTs, NRTs, PLDs, PLCs, Angoff, modified Angoff, genetically modified Angoff, genetically modified, pest-resistant Angoff.

Despite this attempt at humor, Chris's speech, dedicated to Doug, was intended to be a call to keep the faith:

> STARS was a vehicle for good teaching and learning. It was an artist's toolbox. We know—there is no lack of clarity on this point—that STARS, as a policy, no longer remains. But here's the thing: the artists' toolbox remains. And the artists remain. And the vision of effective teaching and learning remains. And the spirit of supporting *all* kids and *all* educators remains.

As it turned out, the speech was a hopeful goodbye. A few months later, for a variety of reasons, not least of which was his sense of loss of connection to K–12 educators, Chris accepted a faculty position at a university in Boston, fourteen hundred miles away.

So both of us walked away—with our values intact. We had lived our values in full view of the people in our corner of world for more than a decade. We had stood up; we could not stand down. We were both heartbroken, especially for the students and teachers who would not know what they had lost and would now have to endure the worst of professional practice in prescriptions from remote places.

The Power of No

At the same time, there is power and hope in *this* refusal, too. First, we say no in honor of STARS and all those who made it a reality. We were blessed to witness firsthand what is possible when we find a better way along the road less traveled. We do not believe STARS was perfect, but we believe it offered an indication of what next-generation assessments and accountability systems might look like. Doug's high school football coach was fond of saying, "When the ball is in your hands, your job is to take it to a better place." Like any running back, Nebraskans faced resistance, and we offered resistance; in the end, we never took our eye off the ball and we moved it to a better place.

We also say no knowing that refusing the right things in the right way at the right time allows us to live our values and deepen our passions. Our work is not over. As teachers and as activists, we will continue to fight for what we and so many of our educational colleagues believe is right. We will continue to speak and write about education and assessment. We will continue to oppose the abuses of centralized and standardized testing and to advocate for better ways of assessing and educating kids. We will continue to support teachers as professionals and students as learners.

This is work to which we—and we hope many of you—can proudly say yes.

Doug Christensen is emeritus commissioner of education for Nebraska, having served fourteen years in that role, and is now professor of leadership in education in the Graduate Division of Doane College. Chris W. Gallagher is professor of English and Writing Program director at Northeastern University.

Note

1. Chris W. Gallagher, "Risking Complexity: Nebraska Teachers as Agents of Reform," *Nebraska English Journal* 45, no. 1 (Spring 2000): 9–20.

9. Why I Quit Teach For America to Fight for Public Education

Neha Singhal

I joined Teach For America (TFA) to make a difference in the lives of students and in the education system. With a passion for social justice education and a degree in business, I thought that TFA seemed like a good place to begin, even though I harbored some doubts about its approach. My experience with the organization only fueled my misgivings about its claim to be a social justice organization fighting to stop educational inequity. Although I resigned from my placement in south Texas after three months for a variety of reasons, I continued to work for immigrant rights in the region for two years.[1]

From my personal experiences and those of friends who completed their two-year commitment with the organization, I gained insights into the corporate-funded education "reform" movement that teachers are up against. I learned how, in contrast to TFA teachers who try to do the best for their students, the organization is trying to control the debate on education reform and influence public policy. Despite its success attracting people who might not have otherwise considered working in K–12 education, the well-funded marketing efforts that portray TFA as the solution to education inequity drown out the negative consequences of the organization's approach, an approach that disregards structural issues and root causes and ignores the poverty and racial inequity that children face every day.

Instead, this free-market approach points to ineffective teachers as the reason for classroom inequity and to high test scores as the solution. The organization also undermines local teachers' ability to obtain jobs and sustain movements for change. Finally, as we peel back the layers and see the relationships among TFA, multinational corporations, politicians, and right-wing foundations, it becomes apparent that TFA is more than just an idealistic two-year teaching program trying to make the world a more equal place for children of color. TFA and its affiliates are trying to influence policy by favoring charter schools, merit-based pay, anti-union policies, and other neoliberal ideas.

How TFA Disregards Root Causes of Educational Inequity

I distinctly remember the excitement I felt when I was accepted to teach high school in the Rio Grande Valley of south Texas at the U.S.-Mexico border. Two thousand miles away from home, I would have the opportunity to combine my passion for immigrant rights and justice in schools. Through community organizing, I had learned that movements for social justice are deeply rooted in history, fueled by grassroots participation, and committed to combating institutional injustice to create long-term systemic change. I looked forward to critical conversations with TFA staff and teachers on how poverty, immigration policy, undocumented status, and other border-specific issues would affect my future students. Since most of us were not from the border area (or even Texas), I imagined that TFA would partner with a local organization to engage teachers to ground us with a better understanding of our students' history and experiences living at the border.

It quickly became clear that we would not be participating in any such activities. Why weren't we discussing institutionalized racism and classism as root causes of the achievement gap? Why were we only focusing on having "good teachers" as the solution? Even during the five-week-long training period, we did not discuss some of fundamental issues regarding education inequity, such as inadequate funding in low-income schools or the impact of high-stakes testing. Nor did we discuss the unique challenges our students face at the U.S.-Mexico border or the repercussions of anti-immigrant policies on families. What kind of civil rights movement is effective without any historical context or participation from the local community, especially when it is led by and primarily consists of those outside the affected community?

The training did not meet my expectations in deconstructing the structural oppression behind educational injustice because TFA does not even acknowledge that these issues exist. Instead, TFA perpetuates a bootstraps mentality: as long as a student works hard, he or she can achieve, regardless of external factors. In order to maintain high expectations of all students, corps members are indirectly told to ignore any societal or historical context informing their students' lives. This policy relieves TFA from the responsibility of tackling complex issues, such as how classism, racism, sexism, and other -isms intersect to have an impact on a child's learning environment. To TFA, this is seen as making excuses for a child; instead, it would have us believe that effective teaching trumps economic and social inequalities.

TFA also steered clear of conversations about multicultural and anti-oppression education in the diversity sessions that all corps members were required to attend. Under the guise of being professional, the diversity sessions taught corps members to stay within their locus of control and not allow external issues to get in the way of effective teaching. During one of these sessions, a corps member asked a question about grappling with his own stereotypes of students of color. I was excited to hear such a brave and important question that would lead us into a rich discussion of privilege and internalized racism, but this inquiry was brushed off with a quick reply as we moved on to another topic. TFA teachers are primarily white and/or from middle- to higher-income backgrounds who have had the opportunity to attain a college degree. They work with students from low-income communities of color, communities that have been historically marginalized and discriminated against. If TFA truly believes in social justice, it would facilitate, instead of discourage, the kind of challenging conversations about internalized stereotypes that would foster a better understanding of power and privilege.

How TFA Undermines Local Teachers and
Long-Term Change in Public Education

One of the reasons I suspect many exalt TFA is the impression that there is a teacher shortage all over the country. While that may be true in some regions, one clear example where this is not the case is the Rio Grande Valley. Before coming to the Rio Grande Valley, I assumed that the schools here were understaffed, and I was helping to ease the effects of a teacher shortage. After meeting local folks and reading the news about many teachers being laid off, I discovered that education is one of the most accessible paths to employment for young people and that hundreds of temporary TFA teachers make it harder for local teachers to obtain long-term careers in education.

Why do certain school districts hire TFA teachers over local ones? The temporary nature of TFA teachers is very appealing for a few reasons: (1) since they will most likely remain for only two or three years, TFA teachers stay at the base salary and are replaced by someone else who will also get the base salary, and so on; (2) TFA teachers are specifically told not to rock the boat and keep a positive relationship between TFA and the district administration. Thus, TFA teachers are appealing to principals because they are unlikely to organize resistance to administrative policies that hurt teachers; (3) TFA teachers are also discouraged from engaging in political activity, allegedly because of AmeriCorps funding, but also because it would threaten TFA's public image of being neutral.

Another major reason is the illusion that TFA teachers get better test scores and are more effective teachers. Many studies have debunked this, but it is important to address the reasons behind these claims. TFA recruits mainly young college graduates who do not have family obligations in the region where they are teaching and are willing to work ten- to fifteen-hour days. Because of the short-term nature of their commitments, TFA teachers do not mind working these unreasonable hours even if it means risking mental health and well-being. I witnessed many teachers struggle with depression and anxiety, finding it difficult to seek support or speak up. TFA also undermines teacher unions in an effort to prove that TFA teachers work harder than local teachers who would find it impossible to carry similar expectations and burdens for the long term.

TFA has also been instrumental in deprofessionalizing teaching as a career path by making it seem as if teachers can learn their profession in a mere five-week training process (mostly staffed by TFA alumni who themselves have taught in the classroom for only a few years). At the policy level, TFA is trying to lower the standards of those considered highly qualified to teach so that TFA teachers in for-profit alternative certificate programs can continue to take jobs in the school system. Since TFA teachers are not adequately trained in pedagogy and, in many cases, content area, I often wonder if parents from higher-income backgrounds would accept having their children taught by noncredentialed college graduates. If not, then why is TFA allowed to teach in working-class communities of color?

TFA and Corporate-Funded, Neoliberal Education "Reform"

If TFA were just an organization that trained teachers to work in understaffed areas of the country, that would be one thing, but the reality is that, at the policy level, TFA is heavily influencing America's whole system of public education. The organization's long-term mission is to support its alumni in solving educational inequity through various careers in public policy, education administration, the government, and corporations. TFA alumni who are actively involved in the education reform debate can usually be spotted by their use of similar language: establish merit pay, end tenure, make it easier to fire teachers, dismantle unions, increase standardized testing, and open more charter schools. Instead of addressing root causes of inequity in our current method of public school funding, the neoliberal policies that TFA alumni support are helping to pave the way to privatized education. Corporate interests that give TFA big money and coveted partnerships are aligned with its emphasis on these free-market ideas as the solution.

TFA also hides behind its 501(c)(3) status, claiming it cannot advocate for broader social justice issues because it is nonpartisan and neutral. In fact, it is in TFA's interest to stay as neutral as possible and stay silent on key issues in order to continue receiving the corporate funding it desperately needs from groups like Goldman Sachs and Walmart. These organizations happily fund TFA efforts because it distracts the public from the real issues that plague our nation's system of education and does not challenge institutionalized racism or classism that corporations are entrenched in and profit from.

Through corporate funding, TFA is paving the way for more privately operated charter schools that divert funding from public schools. While there are a few excellent grassroots charter schools that *are* revolutionizing how students learn, not all charter schools are created equal. The ones that should be scrutinized are those that obstruct workers' rights by operating with rigid rules that nonunionized teachers must follow, such as TFA alumni-created charter schools: IDEA Public Schools, KIPP Academy, and YES Prep. These schools can easily disregard workers' rights because even if local, long-term teachers leave, they can hire temporary TFA teachers. While these charter schools brag about 100 percent graduation rates, the truth is that they can kick students out for a variety of reasons, while public schools cannot.

Our Children Deserve Better

While no one program can solve our education crisis, there are many opportunities for TFA to improve its operations. Instead of spending millions of dollars training temporary teachers, why not invest money to support professional teachers who will build local capacity for change in education? Local teachers are more likely to know their students' culture and stay in their communities to pursue long-term teaching careers that will advance their students' success.

Since resigning from TFA, I have realized that I want to go about becoming a teacher the right way, beginning with a master's program in social justice education, learning the tools and pedagogy an effective teacher needs. While individually, TFA teachers might be able to do great things for their students, TFA as a national organization is harming our system of public education. Those passionate about education should know that there are ways other than joining TFA to get involved in the education reform movement. We can do better for America's children than providing temporary teachers and teaching to the test.

_____

Neha Singhal is an aspiring social justice educator committed to engaging youth in critical analysis of oppression in order to transform and empower themselves and their communities.

Note

1. Neha Singhal's full resignation story is available online at www.debunking tfa.wordpress.com.

10.   Exit Strategies: Confronting Faulty Graduation Tests

Latricia Wilson

My name is Latricia Wilson. I was born in Gary, Indiana, but currently reside in Memphis, Tennessee. I am twenty-five years old and a student at Tennessee Technology Center. Just a few years ago, I wasn't sure if I would be able to achieve any higher education or vocational training because my high school denied me a standard diploma, despite the fact that I had completed all of my courses.

I was denied a proper diploma because I had failed to pass—by a few points—the math section of a new end-of-year test.

The Tennessee Comprehensive Assessment Program (TCAP) Achievement Tests, now called the Gateway exam, are part of the state's assessment program. The high-stakes exit exam I took is part of a growing trend around the country leaving thousands of students without diplomas.

Prior to graduating high school, my career goals were to be a hairstylist and television makeup artist. But after being denied a standard high school diploma in 2002 for failing to pass the TCAP math section, I was denied entry into all beauty schools, even though I was on the technical-vocational path in high school and had taken cosmetology classes during high school. I was also denied entry into other Memphis technical and community colleges and universities.

I struggled as an adult to make a living wage to support myself. I worked as a waitress for years, took on double shifts, and was just barely able to pay my rent. I was getting further away from my career goals and sinking deeper into poverty and debt. Eventually, I was evicted from my apartment. I've truly experienced how difficult it is to be an independent adult without a valid high school diploma.

But I decided to do something about it and started a quest to regain my rightful degree. This is my own experience with Tennessee's public education system and how I was able to change it.

Diploma Drama

I was one of many students denied a high school diploma for failure to pass the TCAP tests in 2002. I had a mild learning disability in math, which made passing those TCAP sections difficult. I had been enrolled in math resource classes from the ninth grade and was instructed at a slightly lower grade level than my classmates. Despite this, I was repeatedly administered the TCAP on a higher grade level than the one at which I was taught. As a result, I was unable to pass the math section by the end of senior year.

I was allowed to participate in the graduation ceremony, but instead of a regular diploma, I received a "special education diploma," awarded to students with physical, emotional, or severe learning disabilities who were not able to meet standard diploma requirements. I was mislabeled for no reason other than having failed the TCAP math section.

Although counselors advised me that I could still further my education, I learned that technical, vocational, and community colleges and universities in Tennessee wouldn't accept my special diploma because these institutions don't consider it a valid graduation certificate. I was shamed and silenced, just like thousands of students who fail these state tests every year.

Gateway's Gaps

Twenty-three states, including Florida, Texas, and California, have adopted exit exams as a requirement for receiving high school diplomas. These assessments might seem like an important way to gauge a school's or student's performance, but in the end they're linked to an inherently flawed public education system that fails to consider factors that hinder student performance, such as lack of access to adequate classroom resources, quality instruction, or tutoring services.

At the time I was in high school, students with learning disabilities were disproportionately affected because Tennessee Public Schools didn't offer reasonable test accommodations, such as portfolio assessments, alternative test formats, or the use of adaptive equipment, even though these are required by federal legislation.

School closures also have an impact on student preparedness for exit exams. In Memphis, for every school that closes, another facility must be made available; otherwise students are assigned to the next closest school. This can lead to class sizes of up to forty students. Overcrowding hinders a teacher's effectiveness in covering core subjects such as English, science, and math. Some teachers aren't even properly prepared to teach the basics.

The Tennessee Department of Education also refuses to release test information that identifies what answers students missed or indicate sections on which they may have performed poorly, thus making it impossible for instructors to help students retaking the Gateway exam.

Denied Opportunities

According to the Tennessee Department of Education Annual Statistical Reports, between 1995 and 2007, a total of 32,233 students statewide were denied standard high school diplomas and given special education diplomas. A further 8,654 students were issued only certificates of attendance (COA).

The Tennessee Department of Education failed to notify students of the COA's limitations, including ineligibility for student loans, scholarships, entrance to the military, or federal Pell Grant funding for postsecondary education, as well as exclusion from technical schools and community colleges and universities.

Students without diplomas earn much less than those in the workforce who have diplomas, and they are less likely to maintain stable families as a result of unemployment or underemployment. They may turn to criminal activities in order to earn an income.

Young people face these challenges every day and the stigma of having failed to complete their education silences them. In my case, it took a lawsuit to regain my voice.

I Had to Do Something

While contemplating my future and feeling frustrated with the system, I decided to appeal the deficiencies of special diplomas and high-stakes exit examination before the Memphis school board and the state legislature and make my case heard on all the Memphis news stations.

I first addressed the Memphis school board at several meetings. Then I began contacting several local and state representatives by e-mail and phone to tell them how graduation requirements had affected my life. I came in contact with Representative Barbara Cooper (D-Tenn.), who at that time was pushing for legislation to change the state graduation policies. She asked me to testify before the House and Higher Education Committee at the Tennessee State Capitol in Nashville.

I also had a one-on-one meeting in Washington, DC, with Congressman Steve Cohen (D-Tenn.). A local blog described the meeting as follows:

> What impressed me about [her] current Congressman is that he didn't blow her off, and when she began to articulate her issue, he immediately offered to put her in touch with the Chairman of the Education sub-committee, Rep. George Miller (D-Calif.). Rep. Cohen gave Ms. Wilson a two-hour meeting on a Friday morning. Expect Latricia to become a "shining star" on the Hill when she gives that testimony before Rep. Miller's subcommittee.[1]

Meanwhile, I approached news reporters while they were covering stories on the streets of Memphis and distributed brief summaries of my personal experience and copies of my diploma.

As a result, a federal class-action lawsuit was filed July 26, 2007, against the Tennessee Department of Education on behalf of all former students who were denied high school diplomas for failure to pass the Gateway exam. Courtney Robinson and I were co-plaintiffs represented by attorney Javier Bailey from the Walter Bailey Law Firm, who filed our case.

Better Days Ahead

Within the lawsuit, my attorney asked the judge to dismantle the Gateway exam as a graduation requirement. We also asked that students denied diplomas be recertified. Unfortunately, the lawsuit was dismissed because of my case's expired statute of limitations. We lost the battle, but in the end we won the war because we were successful as the first case to legally challenge the state on this issue. Tennessee's unfair testing policy had been exposed.

The Tennessee State Board of Education did not want to risk being challenged on graduation testing again, and on January 25, 2008, just a few months after my suit was dismissed, the board moved to eliminate the Gateway exam as a diploma requirement. In the 2009–2010 school year, no student in the state of Tennessee was required to pass any test to qualify for a high school diploma.

While I failed the TCAP math section in 2002 because of systemic failures in the public school system here in Tennessee, I do not consider myself a failure. In fact, I took the Gateway exam on May 1, 2007, in hopes of passing to obtain a standard diploma. I'm determined that I will not be deemed unemployable and incapable of pursuing my career goals merely because of a high school test score.

Latricia Wilson graduated from Tennessee Technology Center with honors and went on to Roosevelt University, where she is pursuing a degree in journalism.

Note

1.   "Getting Rid of the DLC," *The Flypaper Theory*, July 30, 2007, http://thepeskyfly.blogspot.com/.

11. *Tú Eres Mi Otro Yo/*
You Are My Other Self

Curtis Acosta

In Lak Ech

Tú eres mi otro yo / You are my other me.
Si te hago daño a ti / If I do harm to you,
Me hago daño a mí mismo / I do harm to myself;
Si te amo y respeto / If I love and respect you,
Me amo y respeto yo / I love and respect myself.
—Luís Valdez

Each day, my students and I recite this verse from the poem "In Lak Ech," by Chicano writer and activist Luís Valdez.[1] It draws upon our indigenous history, roots, and *cultura*, and reminds us of our common humanity. Through these beautiful words, we are able to reflect upon the true essence of learning and are inspired to roll up our sleeves to help create a better world. With a unified voice, we affirm that teaching, learning, and education must always be about love.

In 2001, as the standardized testing movement exploded upon us in Tucson, Arizona, educators were immediately inundated with professional development that was geared to reeducate and train experienced maestros to be generic teachers. Administrators and district officials expounded on the need for the entire school and district to be in lockstep. Phrases such as "common curriculum" and "pacing calendars" began to take root in our professional discourse, while teacher creativity and innovation were discouraged; teachers could not be trusted to develop curriculum or create educational practices from their own wealth of knowledge, training, and experience.

However, standards have not been the issue for the Raza Studies classes that my colleagues and I teach at Tucson High Magnet

School, since we have maintained a higher degree of expectations for ourselves as teachers than simply teaching to a test. We have been fortunate to see our students make dramatic improvements in their scores on the state's high-stakes assessment, the Arizona Instrument to Measure Standards (AIMS). But more importantly, our students have consistently told us how Raza Studies classes have built an academic identity and desire to continue their education at the college or university level, thoughts that many did not have on the day they entered our classrooms. We believe in a rigorous curriculum that is based upon self-reflection, cultural studies, critical thought, and social justice. We rejected the prepackaged, test-driven curriculum that our district administrators were championing, and we proved that success would follow. We showed that by working in the best interests of the students, not the state, anything is possible. This is our story.

The Context and Origin of Raza Studies'
Educational Revolution

In the Tucson Unified School District (TUSD), we are blessed to have a Mexican American/Raza Studies Department that was created in 1998 from a grassroots community movement. For generations in Tucson, Chicana/o students were often ignored, marginalized, or directly impeded from academic success. The mission for our Mexican American/Raza Studies Department has been to empower students by addressing the educational and academic needs of the Chicana/o community throughout Tucson. It is due to the hard work of youth, parents, educators, and community leaders that we have such a vibrant presence within our schools, fostering the growth of the classes and program.

Nearly a decade ago, as a response to the authoritarian legislation of NCLB, the Mexican American/Raza Studies Department brought together a team of teachers to address the issue and possible effects of the high-stakes standardized test agenda on our students. In our district, art and music classes were discontinued. Schools were demanding that teachers not supplement their curriculum or divert from the standards in any way, which meant a further marginalization of cultural and ethnic history and literature. Initially, even the teaching of poetry was frowned upon, except for those who taught honors or Advanced Placement literature classes. It became clear that we needed a plan to counter such damaging experiences for all our students, and specifically the Chicana/o students.

Tucson High Magnet School (THMS) celebrated its one hundredth anniversary during the 2006–2007 school year. Change does not come quickly to a school with generations of tradition. Thus, the creation of Mexican American/Raza Studies literature and history classes was met with resistance. In team meetings, we eventually developed academic spaces, specific classrooms and classes centered on the Chicana/o experience, at THMS, where I teach English. With Chicana/o literature and studies courses, we focused on rehumanizing the educational experiences for students. Students themselves select Raza Studies classes; on average, the classes are composed of over 90 percent Chicana/o or Latina/o students.

My Chicana/o literature class was created to complement the Chicana/o history class as an academic space that encouraged the authentic exploration of the Mexican American story. The classes specifically attach cultural, historical, and contemporary relevancy to the rigorous and beautiful struggle that is education. This was our response to NCLB, which rolled back the multicultural and pluralistic education movements of the 1980s and 1990s and justified the reinsertion of a less diverse curriculum, all in the name of standards.

Reclaim Your Space: What It Looks Like and How to Get It Done

> The Raza Studies classes created the foundation of my academic, political, and personal life. Throughout my twelve years of public education, I can honestly say that my last two years were the only ones that prepared me for life and not an exam.
>
> —*Arturo Rodríguez, Class of 2008, Gates Millennium Scholar*

In the 2003–2004 school year, my Chicana/o literature class overtly challenged the high-stakes testing movement. I consciously decided to teach reading and writing through a cultural lens with a social justice emphasis, and to disregard the stacks of practice tests that were provided for us. It was essential to reject the dehumanizing approaches that encouraged us to forgo building authentic relationships with our students in order to prepare them for the state test.

As a Raza Studies team, we decided to use cultural and critical literacy to provide a high-quality academic experience, instead of deconstructing our students' lives to results on a test of certain skills. We continued to cultivate an educational experience that had students at the center, while pushing them to improve their academic skills. In short, we changed nothing. All we needed was courage to rebuff the pressures from the district administration. However, since we were starting a new program with new classes from the ground up, the local school administration left us with the academic heavy lifting, emphasizing only one edict: make sure that it complies with the state standards.

We had a blank check and we ran with it. In my classes, I embraced many contemporary Chicana/o writers such as Sandra Cisneros, Luís Valdez, Ana Castillo, and Luís Alberto Urrea. We wanted the classes to be real and reflect what it means to be Chicana/o, so writing assignments were a balance of self-reflection and exploration, along with rhetorical and analytical skills based upon the readings. And since the readings reflected our students' lives and experiences, they were able to continue to develop and grow in consciousness while sharpening their academic writing. We supplemented the curriculum with nonfiction reading from many different social justice perspectives, including critical race theory and the work of Paulo Freire, Jonathan Kozol, and contemporary educational researchers, historians, and sociologists.

What was at the center of our classes was a deep capacity to love one another. This is another area that the high-stakes testing movement disregards and our district deemphasized, but it is essential to Raza Studies classrooms. We have real relationships with one another, beginning from the moment that students walk into our academic spaces. The decorated walls, posters, and art are essential to transforming a school space, which may resemble a primarily negative place for our students, into an academic space that resembles their home, their culture, and their identity. Former student Alexei Moreno wrote, "The information that I was taught in AP English could not compare to the knowledge gained in the Raza Studies literature class. I was finally able to relate to the material being taught. I found myself consumed by characters and authors that reminded me of my family, friends, and even myself."

Our room is filled with pictures ranging from Emiliano Zapata to Frida Kahlo to Angela Davis. From Dolores Huerta to Malcolm X to Che Guevara. An entire wall is dedicated to pictures of alumni and former students who were essential in creating that very space. Student artwork also explodes on the walls of our *chante*, our home.

When administrators come into our room to evaluate my instruction, they often enter with an agenda or discomfort due to the nature of the students' critical dialogue about racism, injustice, and oppression that the literature inspires. As much as the room is inviting to students in our school and community, only a few administrators have felt the same way. However, as administrators and evaluators leave our space, they usually focus on the level of student engagement in the classroom discussion and the work at hand. As Arturo, a student of mine, expressed, "where the classes mean the most to me is in my personal life. The teachers would always find a way to make the struggling students understand the material. Our teachers would not focus on the way we dress, what our first language was, or how we looked; they would always concentrate on our academic needs."

Of course, the scores on a state standardized test for which we had spent no time preparing beyond our own curriculum and pedagogy were the only results that mattered. In 2005, district officials who grumbled about our social justice content and indignant attitude toward high-stakes testing were soon inspired to audit our students' test scores.

However, the gamble to continue to build academic spaces with our students at the center paid off, and the scores eliminated the "achievement gap" between the Chicana/o and Latina/o students in our classes and the European American students in the TUSD. Chicana/o and Latina/o students also dramatically improved and outperformed their peers in the math portion of the exam, although we offer no Mexican American/Raza Studies math class. The only plausible theory for this improvement was that the students began to hope, believe, and see themselves as having an academic identity regardless of the specific disciplines of history, composition, and literature. Many detractors thought these results were a single-year anomaly. However, the scores have been maintained for five years and in four different schools. When asked how we achieved this, Sean Arce, the current director of the Mexican American/Raza Studies Department, said, "We do something revolutionary. We read and write."

Taking Action against Political Attacks

Over the past five years, a small, vicious, and vocal faction of Republican state legislators and officials has aggressively pursued the elimination of the Mexican American Studies department in the TUSD through legislation. We have endured public lambasting by the local conservative radio station, demonizing the teachers and students in our program. My classroom, students, family, colleagues, and I have been the targets as well. Students who were not enrolled in Raza classes have been sent into our space to videotape the classroom decor, students, family pictures, and instruction, and then to upload it to YouTube without our knowledge or consent. Seeing images of my students and family on the Internet in such a context was a chilling experience. These examples are indicative of our times and the degree of unethical behavior some will engage in to maintain the status quo.

Although earlier legislative attempts had proved to be unsuccessful, Arizona HB 2281 was passed and signed into law in the spring of 2010. It allowed the state to fine a school district 10 percent of its funding per month if the state deemed that classes do any of the following:

1. Promote the overthrow of the United States government.

2. Promote resentment toward a race or class of people.

3. Are designed primarily for pupils of a particular ethnic group.

4. Advocate ethnic solidarity instead of the treatment of pupils as individuals.

School district officials and teachers in the program vigorously denied being in violation of any of the language in the law. However, the statute also empowered the Arizona State Superintendent of Public Instruction to be the sole person who can investigate the classes, judge whether there is any violation, and administer the fine upon the school district.

Despite tremendous community support, specifically from the youth of Tucson, who spoke at monthly school board meetings and public forums, the local school district felt intense pressure to eliminate the program in the wake of state officials' threats to fine the district 10 percent of its monthly funding. As the local tension increased, and the fear of losing millions of dollars for our public schools took hold in the community, the Arizona State Superintendent of Public Instruction ordered an extensive audit of our program that included our classrooms and focus groups with teachers, parents, and community members not involved with the Raza Studies program. And despite the auditors' glowing report and analysis of our program and an avalanche of positive testimonies, data, and evidence, the State Superintendent found that our program violated the new law. The truth did not seem to matter, and due to the vagueness of the law and the unprecedented unilateral power it gave to one political figure, the survival of the program faced its most difficult challenge.

Although these incidents and trials have been difficult to endure, we have remained vigilant and strong in the maintenance of our program and classes for the sake of the students and community. As a result of this political situation, three students, ten of my colleagues, and I filed a lawsuit against the state challenging the constitutionality of HB 2281; the legal battle has only begun.

La Lucha Sigue/The Struggle Continues

The past ten years of watching Raza Studies students flourish and the program grow has been like catching lightning in a bottle. Our strength to face the difficult days has come from our collective vision, will, and love for each other and for true educational reform. Teachers are vigilant in finding *compañeros* with creativity, maintaining energy to organize, and taking action to build academic spaces that are geared to the lives and experiences of our students.

Perhaps the experiences in Tucson cannot easily be duplicated in every neighborhood in our country. Educational conditions and political climate are unique, but finding colleagues, community members, and students who are eager for change is the key to reform; communicating clearly with one another, listening closely to the needs of students, while seeking pedagogical approaches and curriculum that will work best for the students will establish a common vision that the entire group will embrace. Students can exceed standards through a myriad of academic experiences; a one-size-fits-all approach does not work. Teachers must be aware of the knowledge in their community, the lives of their students, and use their craft as a foundation for reflection and change.

The process and the product will be students who reflect the best of public education in our country and who see themselves as their sister's and brother's keeper and as a vital piece in creating a more just world. They will be young people who possess critical thought and consciousness and the desire to be active voices for change, and will build a more critical democracy. Believe it is possible. *Sí, se puede!*

Curtis Acosta is proud of the love and commitment of his family and students in developing one of the most dynamic chapters in Mexican American educational history.

Note

1. Luís Valdez, *Early Works: Actos, Bernabe and Pensamiento Serpentine* (Houston: Arte Público Press, 1990).

Part III

Introduction: Resisting by "Working in the Cracks"—Creating Spaces to Teach Authentically

Has there ever been a time in your life when you've been in a challenging situation—one that didn't reflect your values—but you stuck with it anyway? Perhaps you found ways to carve out spaces to act with integrity, ways to challenge the system while remaining a part of it. This is another way to resist a hurtful system, by not giving up, being persistent, and using your creativity to foster what change you can. The narratives that follow describe ways educators have resisted market-driven educational policies by "working in the cracks."

These narratives delineate many ways that teachers and administrators have acted imaginatively and boldly—even within a test-driven context—to develop students' intellectual, social, and emotional learning, and to educate the whole child. With a clear commitment to social justice education, they enable their students to explore the social context of their lives, empowering them to understand how racism, sexism, and other forms of social inequality affect them and how they can contribute to change. To accomplish this, educators must press against the boundaries of neoliberal educational expectations.

Some teachers have been able to write innovative curricula that integrate their own best thinking with what's expected on the test. In some cases, principals have acted as shields to protect teachers from test-driven policies and practices, creating more cracks in which educators can teach authentically.

Given that test scores often have such high-stakes consequences for students, teachers have struggled with ways to integrate meaningful content with the understanding and skills that are needed to be successful on the tests. Ellen Davidson worked with teachers to analyze tests and then developed social justice–based curriculum that teaches such needed skills. She points out that the teachers she worked with had privileges that teachers in most other districts don't have—staff development time, resources, and principal support.

Jessica Klonsky describes a nonfiction writing curriculum about "a topic my students were hungry to understand" in preparation for the New York State Regents test, a high school exit exam. Her unit on the war in Iraq integrated not only skills for writing the nonfiction essay on the Regents exam, but critical media literacy skills that also taught students to recognize distortions, omissions, and lies in the mainstream media.

The degrees of freedom teachers have to work in the cracks vary tremendously. Some might think, "If these teachers can develop curriculum that is meaningful, then all teachers can. If teachers don't rise to the occasion, it's their problem." This argument belies the reality of life in schools. While some teachers have pedagogical freedom to teach to the standards and tests in a way they choose, many others do not. Especially in urban schools or schools that educate low-income children, a rote curriculum is often dictated. In some schools, all teachers must be on the same page of the same curriculum at the same hour on the same day, and they are monitored accordingly. Teachers who typically teach white, more economically privileged students are often given more flexibility. These different approaches to curriculum and instruction have an impact on not only immediate student learning, but also the development of a rich knowledge base and critical thinking skills that affect what types of work they can aspire to as adults.

Educators are also able to work within the cracks by raising students' consciousness about the problematic nature of the tests so students don't blame themselves for low scores or feel superior for high scores. Many teachers impress upon students that standardized tests don't accurately assess all they know or show the multiple ways that they are smart. The National Council of Teachers of English helped parents put testing in its place through the distribution of buttons and bumper stickers that read, "My Child is More than a Test Score!"

School principals can play a major role in creating space for teachers to work in the cracks. They can be buffers that shield teachers from test pressures or hammers that pound away at teachers' autonomy with testing mandates. Recognizing that the "transcending purpose of schools is to heal and transform lives," Felipa Gaudet's principal created the space for Felipa and her kindergarten class to address the trauma of one student, Ivory, whose story Felipa tells. Had her principal forced her to conform to rigid benchmark targets, at the exclusion of curriculum that springs from the children, this child would have been denied the opportunity to heal and to learn.

Tom Roderick's interview with principal Christina Fuentes of P.S. 24 in New York City demonstrates how leadership and persistent efforts can confront barriers that current federal, state, and city policies throw in the way of educators committed to giving low-income children of color the education they deserve. When her school was labeled a "school in need of improvement," Fuentes could have responded by making test-prep the top priority. Rather, she and her faculty, through time-consuming grant-writing and partnering with other organizations, sustained this public school's parental involvement, professional development, social and emotional learning, dual-language instruction, and arts education. Fuentes reminds us, "You can't be driven by fear. . . . I'm not going to compromise my deepest convictions. Those convictions are why I do what I do. They're what keep me going."

Of course, teachers shouldn't *have to* work in the cracks. Rather than responding to top-down mandates, teachers could be teaching toward, and assessing, educational goals using a curriculum that's meaningful to their students. But when educators work in the cracks, they often widen those cracks. What's small can become large. It's important to think about how we can support those sites of resistance.

Another site of resistance is found in alternative schools within the public school system that have, in the face of neoliberal policies, maintained long-term quality programs with democratic practices and values. In these schools, teaching, learning, and assessment are student centered. Why do we need to create charter schools, with their various degrees of connection to private corporations and foundations, when schools for innovation can be supported *within* the public school system? In the late 1960s and 1970s, there were hundreds of alternative public schools in school districts across the country. Often small, with curricular flexibility, some developed to meet the needs of specific communities and communities of color. These schools promoted innovations that fostered academic, social, and multicultural learning and enriched both their students and the districts they were part of. Teacher Bette Gobeille Diem describes, on the *Educational Courage* website (www.beacon.org/educational courage), her work with the Ann Arbor Open School, one of the noteworthy alternative public schools that exist today.

Our hope is that even though many of the educators whose narratives you read here may have had funding or personal support that others didn't, their pieces will provide ideas for resistance by creating spaces for authentic teaching and learning, whatever the educational context. We hope that teachers will gain encouragement and courage by seeking out other educators who are working in the cracks, thus creating networks of cracks that will ultimately create many spaces of resistance for meaningful learning.

12. Deepening the Cracks to Infuse Mathematics for Social Justice

Ellen Davidson

Teaching continues to be an increasingly challenging profession as teachers work toward addressing the educational needs of their students while at the same time teaching in a way that helps students score well on their state's high-stakes test. Clearly there are times when these goals are in conflict, and teachers, principals, and other administrators make instructional decisions about time and money. I have had the good fortune to work in districts that, although they have high percentages of low-income students, have been able to find the funding to support teachers and learners in developing the *content* of mathematics.

In Massachusetts, our test is known as MCAS (the Massachusetts Comprehensive Assessment System), one of the most rigorous and most conceptual of the standardized tests. Although the MCAS may be better than some other state tests, it still has major flaws. In its favor, the MCAS is untimed. Perhaps controversially, in addition to having multiple-choice items, at all grade levels there are a significant number of short-answer and open-response questions that are designed to test the depth of children's understanding. This can cause problems for English-language learners (ELLs), especially those whose parents haven't had access to higher education themselves. I work with ELLs who come from highly educated families with parental mathematical knowledge and access to outside-of-school mathematics instruction, and they do just as well in MCAS testing as those students who speak English at home. This is not the case for most students.

As a college professor in mathematics education and a consultant in local public schools, I work together with teachers to address the dilemma of how to teach effectively while also preparing students for the MCAS. Fortunately, we located materials relatively easily so that we don't need to invent everything ourselves. There is extensive multicultural information available on the Internet, and relevant children's picture books and chapter books are also easy to find. Our job then is to take these ideas and adapt them to ensure we are teaching the necessary content and style of thinking for the mathematics MCAS.

The examples I describe next are from my experiences working in second through sixth grades in both the Brookline and Boston public schools. In these examples, working in the cracks clearly involves more work on the part of teachers and also allows for more of their creativity. As we work, we push the boundaries and widen the cracks, thus fitting in more and more of the kinds of mathematics learning we think are essential for our students. Much to our relief, we have found many ways to teach that allow us to go back to *why* we decided to become teachers in the first place: our commitment to helping *all* children genuinely develop academic and social skills that will serve them well now and throughout their lives. Clearly, this work is much easier because we have the privilege of working for principals in schools that actively support this approach with allocations of time and money.

Some of these examples are short term, taking only a day or two of instructional time and focusing on a narrow range of mathematical skills. Other examples are more involved, fully or close to fully teaching a particular mathematical strand through a social justice lens. For these, a teacher might take the unit in the mathematics text and teach each lesson within a chosen social justice context.

A third version is a classroom project, often embedded in the context of what is being studied in social studies or science, where the mathematics is used as a tool, carefully structured to simultaneously help with the content of the subject and with important mathematics.

Learning Large-Number Computation
While Helping the Environment

Ms. Stark was listening to her students' conversation about the noise from endless leaf blowing right outside their classroom window and thinking about the MCAS practice she needed to be doing with them in mathematics. She knew that, in order to do well on this test, they needed more facility working with and understanding large numbers, and doing computation *in context* with large numbers. This was the third time the class had been interrupted by leaf blowing in the last three weeks. Students complained that the leaf blowers were using gasoline, polluting the environment, and making noise. Ms. Stark realized her students were ready to *do something* about it. She also quickly realized their energy for environmental concerns could be harnessed into instruction in mathematics as well as into social action. So began the "Green Math Action Plan."

Over the next few days, the students brainstormed on their environmental concerns. Students chose which topic interested them the most and began their group work. In order to structure the work, Ms. Stark created an overall worksheet, Green Math Action Plan. Under the title "Cafeteria Tray Questions," the teacher asked: How much do Styrofoam trays cost? How much do plastic trays cost? How much would hot water and staff time cost if we used plastic trays and washed them? What is the environmental impact of producing plastic trays? Are there other alternatives?

The small-group work began. One of the most mathematically complicated projects was on the use of disposable Styrofoam trays in the cafeteria. Generating their list of questions involved complex thinking about all the factors that they needed to consider. This group conducted interviews and did Internet research. They compared the cost of disposable trays to the cost of washing trays. All this work necessitated careful research; a great deal of computation, especially using multiplication and division; and real-world exposure to large numbers.

Another group of students looked at overall paper use in the school. They first filled in their Green Math Action Plan. The plan asked them to describe the project they were working on, the school's current situation regarding the project, the questions that the group members had about the project, and how they were going to find the answers. They were then asked to describe the math they needed to do the project. By the end of this unit, the students realized they were not going to be able to accomplish all they hoped to during that school year. Not discouraged, they ended their work on the unit with a plan for more work to do the next year, perhaps by them, or perhaps by the incoming fourth graders.

Using Mathematics to Understand History Better

The third-grade team and I met in early January to discuss the next few units in the mathematics textbook. The team had been evaluating which strands in mathematics needed more work based on what was expected for the third-grade MCAS. One area, typical for third grade, was the need for more fluency in multidigit addition and subtraction. Another area was continued growth in understanding numbers larger than three digits.

In January, in social studies and language arts, the third graders were heavily focused on learning about Martin Luther King Jr. The word problems for math class were designed for several purposes. One was to practice the mathematics skills needed, which included working with large numbers, multidigit addition and subtraction, and solving word problems with a variety of operations, including multistep word problems. Another purpose was to help children avoid seeing Martin Luther King Jr. as a hero who worked *in isolation* but rather to see him as part of a *movement* that succeeded because so many people worked collaboratively. The word problems were created to support content taught in social studies and language arts, as well as to challenge some of the myths around King and to teach children about a broader range of people involved in the civil rights movement at this time. The problems were equally carefully designed to give children an opportunity for the work they needed to do for their own mathematical learning as well as for success on their upcoming MCAS testing.

One question read:

One of the main organizers of the Bus Boycott was Jo Ann Robinson, a Black woman who had been active in the Civil Rights movement for many years. On the evening of December 1, 1955, after Rosa Parks had refused to move to the back of the bus, Jo Ann Robinson made 35,000 copies of a flyer asking Blacks to boycott the buses for *one day*. She and her students gave out the flyers all over Montgomery. There are 500 sheets of paper in a package and 10 packages in a big box of paper. How many boxes of paper did they use to make all these copies?

Multicultural Mathematics Problems

Velina and her younger brother are sent to the river to get water. Velina has a calabash that holds exactly seven quarts of water. Her brother has one that holds exactly five quarts. Their fussy mother has told them to come back home with exactly one quart of water. They know that she will be upset if they don't do this right. How do they do this? (Since they are using calabashes, their containers aren't transparent and aren't regular shapes nor are they exactly the same shape or weight as each other.)

Nasser and Aviva are working on a cooperative Jewish-Palestinian irrigation project in Israel. It takes Nasser two hours to dig fifty meters of the ditch and it takes Aviva four hours to dig the same length ditch. If the two of them work together, each having their own shovels and each working the whole time as efficiently as they work alone, how long will it take them to dig fifty meters?

One of our commitments is to be sure that when we create our own word problems, they are problems of high cognitive demand—problems that necessitate deep and careful mathematical thinking, not just ones where students can "plug in" formulas or procedures. We also check these problems carefully to see what messages are imbedded in them and if these are the messages we want to convey. The box "Multicultural Mathematics Problems" has some samples of multicultural problems we've used in our classrooms. In most cases, the actual mathematics problems came from other sources, including standard textbooks. Our work has involved giving these problems a new context and, thus, a new life.

The context of the following word problem allowed our students to work with similar kinds of fractions as on the MCAS but in a context of social justice:

> Each month Mary works long hours on several house-cleaning and babysitting jobs. She carefully supports herself and her three children on this money. She spends 1/5 of it on food. She spends 3/8 of what remains on monthly bills such as utilities, telephone, medical expenses, and transportation. She spends 7/10 of what is now left for rent, and 1/3 of the money that remains after that to pay back her mother from whom she had borrowed money when she needed a security deposit in order to be able to rent her current apartment. After all that, she is left with $100 for clothes, contributions to her church, school expenses for her children, entertainment, and so forth. How much money does she start out with each month?

Service Learning

Ms. Doubilet's second graders were studying Ghana. They were fascinated by the lives of children in Ghana and were readily embracing the idea of understanding similarities and differences. One of their overriding concerns was the schooling in Ghana and the privileges that they, in Massachusetts, had that the children in Ghana didn't have. The children eagerly became involved in a service learning project of raising money for a school in Ghana. They obtained a large quantity of Ghanaian painted glass beads and made bracelets, necklaces, and key chains to sell.

One of the biggest challenges was how to choose prices for these items that everyone agreed were sensible—high enough to raise a good amount of money, low enough so people would buy the items. This experience, which worked toward a genuine goal of reaching decisions on pricing, gave these children early exposure to mode, mean, and median, important mathematical skills in real life and on the MCAS tests.

The children sorted money and figured out different strategies for counting it at the end of each day. At the end of the five days of their craft fair, they added up each day's total sales for their grand total of $800 to donate to the Ho Airfield Primary School in Ghana.

Data and Statistics

Occasionally we do all-school mathematics projects. One very successful project was based on the book *If the World Were a Village* by David Smith. This allowed us to teach graphing, relevant for the MCAS starting in grade three, as well as to teach about world resource distribution.

In the younger grades, students acted out how wealth is currently shared in the world by representing the wealth of a village of a hundred people with one hundred cookies. Attempting to distribute one hundred cookies fairly among forty or fifty first, second, and fourth graders took a little calculating. The children figured out that each child would get exactly two whole cookies in a group of fifty or, trickier, a fair share of two-and-a-half cookies in a group of forty. But the world is not fair. Therefore, using the book's statistics—that in a real-world village of one hundred, the majority of the "riches" would be distributed among just a few, while an almost equal number of villagers would receive almost nothing, with the majority falling somewhere in between; we attempted to reflect that calculation with the cookies. Second graders made a graph to represent these findings using handprints and paper cookies.

Fourth graders explored how to graph the distribution of world wealth in percentages. We found out that if the world had a hundred people and wealth were distributed as it is now, six people would own 59 percent, seventy-four people would own 39 percent, and twenty people would share the remaining 2 percent.

Sixth graders used additional data from the book to explore world languages. They also added census data about languages spoken at home in the United States and primary languages of school families in our district. The mathematical thrust here was on understanding the relationship between bar graphs and pie graphs. Students worked in pairs to take one set of data and graph it in two ways—a bar graph and then a pie graph.

As teachers, we began our work together by squeezing social justice teaching practice into bits of cracks as we found them. Then we discovered that the more we pushed on the edges of the cracks, the wider we could make them. Clearly, we need to collaborate; the more we work together, the better our ideas, and the harder we can push, thus opening wider and wider cracks. We need active support from school administrators. This support needs to be in terms of priorities, money, and investment of teacher time. The work is difficult and time consuming—and we shouldn't have to do it—but it can also be productive as we see our students greatly increasing their knowledge of diversity and social justice and mathematics, while also raising their MCAS scores.

<hr>

Ellen Davidson is associate professor of practice in the Education Department at Simmons College.

13. Test Prep and the War

Jessica Klonsky

"You continue saying 'we.' Who is 'we' when you are not fighting in Iraq yourself?"

"We have many weapons. Do you feel it would be right for another country to disarm us?"

"If we ignored Saddam Hussein's use of chemical weapons in the past, why do we care now when he isn't using them?"

My students asked these questions—more difficult than those posed by the U.S. media—during a role play in which I pretended to be President George W. Bush giving his 2003 State of the Union address a few months before the United States invaded Iraq.

The mock press conference was part of a unit in which I blended studying about the war with preparing my students for the New York State English Language Arts Regents Exam, which they must pass in order to graduate. Despite the usual misgivings about what I could and should have done better, I felt pleased that I had been able to meld such an important topic with the district's impossible-to-avoid curricular focus on test prep.

I teach eleventh-grade English in Brooklyn at a high school serving a low-income, predominantly Latino population. Every year, I have to prepare my students, many of whom are English-language learners (ELLs), for the Regents Exam. Because half of the exam is based on nonfiction writing, I decided to create a nonfiction unit that focused on the war but that would also allow my students to practice skills they need for the Regents in summarizing, annotating, note taking, and responding to nonfiction writing.

The first day of what became an almost monthlong unit, I asked students to write down everything they knew about the war. We then shared the writings aloud, giving me a sense of the students' level of understanding. Some students thought Iraq was responsible for the

9/11 attacks, while others knew that Osama bin Laden had no relationship with Iraq. Some didn't even know where Iraq was.

Overall, students were overwhelmingly against the war and hostile toward the Bush administration. At the same time, a number were considering joining the military after high school and would undoubtedly end up in Iraq. I felt I had a responsibility to ensure that they would be able to make informed choices about their future after high school.

In almost all of my classes, three reasons for being in Iraq showed up on the students' lists: (1) we are bringing democracy to Iraq; (2) we are stopping terrorism and getting rid of weapons of mass destruction; and (3) our government wants oil and political control over the Middle East. Before we examined those different reasons, I wanted to address the issue of the media, in particular, how to determine whether a news source is reliable.

I asked my students, "How do we know when we are getting the full picture?" I was surprised by the frustration and cynicism in many of their answers: "You can't believe anything the television tells you." "The president says this and somebody else says that. It's impossible to know who to believe."

It was clear that my students needed to see that it was possible to critically evaluate the information they received and to develop informed opinions about the war. I also wanted them to acquire an understanding of the history and politics that led to the war, so they would be aware of the distortions, omissions, and outright lies in much of the U.S. mainstream media coverage.

Summarizing Different Viewpoints

One of the most successful media-related lessons involved an exercise in which we compared two media viewpoints. First, I showed the first twenty minutes of *Control Room*, a documentary about Al-Jazeera, the international Arabic-language television network headquartered in Doha, Qatar. Students were shocked by the dead bodies and destruction shown on Al-Jazeera. For many, it was the first time they realized that it wasn't just soldiers who died in war.

For homework, students were to find a U.S. newspaper story about the war and summarize it using the "someone-wants-but-so" strategy—a summarizing strategy in which students create a string of sentences in order to summarize a text. This strategy requires students to identify the "main player" in a piece of writing (the "someone"), his or her motivation ("wants"), the conflict ("but"), and the resolution ("so"). Summarizing in this way was useful for preparing students for the upcoming exam, where they would have to summarize unfamiliar information in an essay.

In the following class, we discussed how the viewpoints differed, with students comparing Al-Jazeera with the U.S. newspapers in terms of whose lives and interests were advanced. My goal was not for students to decide that Al-Jazeera was either a better or worse news source than the *New York Daily News* or the Fox Broadcasting Company. Rather, I wanted my students to see that the news we are regularly exposed to is not telling the "whole story" about the war.

Annotating Background Information

It was clear from our look at the news media that my students needed additional background information. I adapted an exercise from *Whose Wars? Teaching About the Iraq War and the War on Terrorism* by Rethinking Schools, on the history of Iraq-U.S. relations. I shortened the selection of situations from ten to six and simplified the language for my ELL students.

Working in pairs, students read each situation and selected the response they thought the U.S. government should take from a list ranging from "use military force" to "officially criticize actions" to "support with economic and humanitarian aid." I made it clear that I did not want them to decide what our government would most likely do but, rather, what they thought was the right thing to do. I gave the students a brief explanatory paragraph for each situation, and students annotated each paragraph, underlining key ideas and writing their thoughts and questions in the margins. This kind of careful annotation is an important strategy for students when taking the Regents Exam.

The next day, I gave students a one-page document with the actual U.S. responses. We went over these as a class, and students continued to annotate. Even with simplified language and working in pairs, many of the less-skilled readers had enormous difficulty working through these adapted texts. With little or no prior knowledge of Middle Eastern history, nor much experience untangling complex geopolitical situations, many of my students struggled to understand the various interactions among Iran, Iraq, Saudi Arabia, and the United States over the past twenty-five years. Even so, students drew some important conclusions from trying to decide the right choice for the United States to make in each situation.

Afterward, students wrote in-class personal responses, choosing from a list of questions I provided, such as: How has U.S. policy in Iraq been consistent or inconsistent? How do the U.S. government decisions of the past help you answer the questions you have about the current war?

Note Taking and Questioning

One of the most interesting activities involved watching the documentary film *Fahrenheit 9/11* by Michael Moore. Politically, the documentary not only provided additional background information but addressed the question of whether the U.S. government's interests are the same as the interests of people living in the United States. Academically, it provided a chance to improve student skills in note taking and questioning.

As the students watched the film, they kept notes on a graphic organizer I had provided for them. In particular, I had students keep notes on memorable lines from either Moore or the people he interviewed. Because part of the Regents Exam requires students to take notes on a passage read aloud to them (but that they never get to read themselves), this note-taking practice was especially important.

Afterward, I put some of the lines they selected (along with some of my own) on pieces of chart paper that I put up around the room (another exercise from *Whose Wars?*). I read aloud each quote and then passed out Post-it Notes. The students went through a few rounds of responding to the quotes with their Post-its, and then responding to each other's responses, all without speaking. Later, I opened up a class discussion by asking for students to speak on anything they had read that struck them deeply. Depending on the class, these discussions spanned a number of topics—from concerns about military recruitment to whether things would be different if we had a black president.

Fahrenheit 9/11 is a great film for bringing up issues around the causes and the consequences of the war. It lays out and documents, with real people and actual corporations, the ways in which this war had been waged to profit the few at the expense of the many. However, I wanted my students to develop a critical eye toward sources of information on the war, even ones they might be sympathetic to.

Toward that end, we spent a few class periods looking at logical fallacies such as slippery slope, red herring, and the straw-man argument. We practiced identifying these fallacies in a number of non-Iraq-war-related examples, and then I asked them to think back on the documentary to identify any logical fallacies.

They quickly identified the ad hominem attacks in the form of cheap shots and still photos of the president looking awkward. They saw Moore's mockery of smaller and less powerful countries involved in the "Coalition of the Willing" as a red herring. One student noted that Moore conveniently left out Great Britain from his list of countries in the coalition—a fallacy of omission.

Before moving on to the unit's culminating exercise—a mock Regents Exam essay—it was time for the students to hear from the president himself.

In another exercise from *Whose Wars?* I pretended I was the president and my students were the media. They listened to me read the 2003 State of the Union address while they had a copy in front of them. In the press conference that followed, they asked me questions. In responding, I tried to use a number of logical fallacies, including some from Bush's actual State of the Union speech.

The students thoroughly enjoyed "grilling" the president, but were also frustrated by their inability to get straight answers. After the press conference, students wrote in-class response papers about their thoughts and opinions on the war. Before the unit began, most were against the war and critical of Bush. But now their opinions were based on a more solid understanding of the war and the history of U.S.-Iraq relations.

As one student wrote, "[This unit] has opened up a whole new thing to me, because before I even saw the video [*Fahrenheit 9/11*] on Iraq I was interested, but not as much as I am now. I mean, when I heard that they were bombing Iraq, I didn't realize the deaths and pain the women and children were going through. It opened my eyes."

Writing Exam Essays

To end the unit, I created a mock Regents Exam essay assignment, in which students read a nonfiction essay, examined a chart or graph, and then responded to show that they understood what they had read. Using the format of countless Regents essay exams I had seen over the years, I created this situation:

> *The students in your class are presenting information to each other about the current war in Iraq. To prepare the class with information on different aspects of the war, your teacher has asked each student to write a report explaining a specific aspect of the war.*

In groups of three or four, students selected a specific topic about the war from a list that included cultural-ethnic tensions in Iraq, the role of oil, and military recruitment. Each group received an article and a map, chart, or graph about their topic. To understand the materials, students used the summarizing, annotating, note taking, and questioning techniques we had practiced throughout the unit. Based on this information, they then individually crafted a straightforward informational essay.

In some ways, the essay was a letdown as a final assignment because the Regents essay format does not allow for students to express their own opinions or to bring in much outside knowledge, which leads to drab, formulaic writing. I generally felt good about the content of what we had studied in the unit and that my students had been able to practice important skills such as summarizing, note taking, and annotation. Yet I realized the unit had shortcomings in preparing students for the Regents Exam. Clearly, blending important curricular content with a prepackaged high-stakes test is not easy.

The exam requires students to read a nonfiction passage on a topic about which they might not have any prior knowledge. In our unit, however, students studied and then wrote about the same topic. While this undoubtedly helped students develop their reading comprehension skills, I wondered if it would help them write about possible topics on the Regents essay, such as irrigation. Or the history of vaudeville theatre. Or manatees.

Indeed, in this unit, my students had the luxury to write about something they cared about and had studied—rather than the Regents approach of writing on something you may care nothing about or know nothing about, and do so for ninety minutes. This, of course, brings up the question of what is most important to know how to do before graduating high school.

Overall, I felt this unit engaged students on a topic they were hungry to understand. When I compared their questions at the beginning of the unit to their questions for Bush during the press conference, I saw how they moved from general distrust and cynicism toward very specific questions that showed a more in-depth understanding of the war. And such specificity is essential to overcome generalized feelings of cynicism and hopelessness, not just about the war but other issues such as racism and poverty that the war exposes. Being able to understand history as it unfolds helps students think about how things might be different and what would need to be done to make changes.

I hope that detailing my experiences with this unit will encourage other teachers to share their ways of dealing with the dreariness of test prep, while still keeping their teaching vibrant and their curriculum relevant.

Jessica Klonsky teaches English at International High School in Prospect Heights, Brooklyn, New York.

References
Al Jazeera, http://english.aljazeera.net
Control Room (Lions Gate, 2003)
Fahrenheit 9/11 (Sony Pictures, 2003)
National Priorities Project, http://nationalpriorities.org
Whose Wars? Teaching about the Iraq War and the War on Terrorism
    (Milwaukee, WI: Rethinking Schools, 2006)

14. Alligator-Crocodile

Felipa Gaudet

Imagine a world in which a child's cry receives no comfort, no validation. In that imagined world, the teacher has neither the time nor the permission to attend to a child in crisis. What would be the repercussions not only for that child and teacher, but also for society's collective future?

When I tell people that I teach kindergarten, they often share their fondest recollections of that time in their lives; they share stories of strong social and community connections. Sadly, their memories would contrast sharply with the reality of today's kindergartens. Because of increased standardized testing within elementary grades, most districts are creating strict benchmark targets for even the youngest children in our schools. As a result, many kindergartners now spend the majority of their time completing meaningless worksheets that their teachers hope will improve their academic performance. While all students experience the negative effects of these changes, children who have experienced trauma are the most at risk of failure within such environments.

Fortunately, I have not been forced to sacrifice my young students' social and emotional welfare to "teach to the test." I owe this freedom to my principal, whose fortitude has provided a refuge from mounting testing pressures. Without her courage and conviction, I would be unable to share the following story. This is a story of the transformative power of schools—a power only possible when students' well-being is valued more than narrow testing targets.

It was morning meeting on a bitter cold and dry January morning. Sunlight streamed through the windows illuminating the colorful faces of twenty-one kindergartners. Ivory, a round girl with a face the shape of a diamond and the color of rich, sweet toffee, had shoulder-length, wavy brown hair that gently rested on her shoulders. Sometimes, Ivory's left eye wandered when she was feeling bothered, but, today, her soft brown eyes were focused intently. This morning, Ivory sat in front of the Nature Garden, a long, shallow, wooden tray that held an assortment of artifacts that the children had discovered in nature. I thought to myself, "Wow, she has come a long way!" remembering a time only a few months earlier when she could not control the urge to pick up the pumpkins and gourds and throw them down as hard as she could. "Gentle" was the message then, "Gentle." Now, she sat with her hands in her lap in front of the delightfully tempting structure, demonstrating her emerging sense of self-control.

As we were reading the day's agenda, Ivory raised her hand high, her lips pressed tightly together. She informed the class that she had a new center for everyone to share. Ivory began to teach the children how to use her new center. She sat in the place usually reserved for the teacher, and I took my place beside her. In her hand, she held her pink fleece hat. Within its soft interior lay her "alligator-crocodile." She began by describing her treasure: "This is my alligator-crocodile."

In a soft-toned, yet confident voice, Ivory instructed the children about the proper care of her creature.

"If you want to touch him, that means you have to take off my hat, gently like this." She carefully slid the alligator-crocodile from the soft confines of her fleece hat. "If you want to carry him, that means you have to carry him like this, like a baby." She cradled her sharp-toothed creature in her arms.

"You have to be soft with him." She ran her hand softly down the alligator-crocodile's back.

As Ivory spoke, I was struck by her speech and demeanor, so different from the girl who had first stepped foot in our school three months earlier. As I had checked my mail in the office one October morning, I heard a woman's voice saying, "Remember: no kicking, no punching, and no bad words." I turned to see a slightly disheveled little girl, her round belly peeking out of the bottom of her shirt; she clung to the side of a woman, whom I would later learn was her stepmother, Alanna. With streams of tears rolling down her cheeks, Ivory cried that she was afraid to go to school because she did not want to sit in time-out. When I reassured her that she would not have to do so, she reluctantly left the safety of her stepmother's side, took my hand, and walked to her new classroom.

Later that day—and for months that followed—Ivory could not uphold her promise to Alanna. She not only kicked, punched, and yelled bad words; she also pushed, spit, threw things, scratched, stomped, screamed, and sobbed. Each day, I left school physically and emotionally exhausted.

Within the safe parameters of dramatic play, Ivory had revealed the traumatic events of her life, helping me to better understand her behavior. Using a baby to represent herself, Ivory repeatedly enacted the physical abuse that she had endured. Just prior to her entry into our school, Ivory had been removed from her biological mother's home because she had been beaten so badly that she was hospitalized for a week. Shortly thereafter, she had to leave everyone and everything that had been familiar to her when she traveled across the country to live with her father and stepmother.

During those first weeks, Ivory was often a cat when she entered our classroom in the mornings. She did not talk. She only scratched and hissed. One day during meeting time, Ivory scratched Samuel. As was the standard practice for dealing with conflicts in our class, he gave her an "I feel" message. He looked into her stony eyes and said, "I feel sad when you scratch me hard. I want you to scratch me softly." Her face softened. "You want me to scratch you softly?" she asked, a little surprised. "Yes," he replied. "Okay," she agreed. As simple as it was, Samuel's solution for Ivory respected her need to be a cat. I thought about what I would have chosen had I intervened. Like Samuel's, my adult solution would have stated the message of respect for his physical being, but unlike his solution, mine would have lost the message of respect for Ivory to be a cat. Innately, Samuel knew that Ivory needed to be a cat. Her imaginary claws and teeth guaranteed protection. Nobody could hurt her if she was a cat. Samuel sat beside Ivory again. She scratched his hand softly and he laughed that it tickled. The outcome of their conflict strengthened their friendship. Samuel gave Ivory the message that she was a part of his world—he just wanted her to be softer. She learned that she could be a soft kitten, still possessing her claws and teeth, but she did not have to use them.

A few months ago, Ivory had been a cat. On this cold January day, she was the baby alligator-crocodile, a small creature with sharp teeth that needed to be loved and treated properly. Ivory guarded her alligator-crocodile with vigilance, just as she herself needed protection.

"So, you have to take care of him," Ivory continued. "If you want to touch him, that means you put him down. But, if I see you doing . . . if I see you biting him, that means that I have to put him back to my backpack." Again, she softly demonstrated how to pet her alligator-crocodile. "Only, you can do this. But, just not like this." She yanked the creature's arm. "If I see you breaking him like that, that means I have to take him back."

Emily called out, but Ivory placed her index finger over her tightly pressed lips, while forming the quiet symbol with her other hand. "*Wow! That is exactly what I do when someone calls out,*" I thought to myself.

She chose Marc, who had raised his hand. "Um, I know the rule, but don't break it because Alanna will get very mad."

Ivory conveyed the seriousness of the situation. "Nope. She'll be not very mad. She'll be very, very, very, *very,* very mad and she'll be very, very, very, very sad. And she'll cry . . ."

Through Ivory's lesson, I could see past her scratchy exterior into her vulnerable heart. She had deeply sensed Alanna's anger and sadness over the abuse that had been inflicted upon her stepdaughter.

When Ivory was satisfied with her classmates' understanding of the alligator-crocodile's care, she declared: "So now we're ready for centers."

At once, the children started asking Ivory questions.

She looked at the class with the same serious teacher face that I had reserved for such occasions and rewarded the desired behavior,

"Oh, oh, oh. Some of us raising our hand. So, I picked Marc already. So, I'll pick one at a time first. I'll pick Jengo."

"The children listen to her better than they listen to me," I marveled to myself. Jengo assured Ivory, "I'll make sure for you everybody is taking care of the crocodile." Despite his kind offer to help, Ivory wanted to be the alligator-crocodile's sole protector. "No. You're gonna pick a center. I'm not. I'm not gonna play a center today. I'm gonna watch all the kids. If I see dramatic play pulling the hands that means that I'll be very mad and Alanna will see it broken. Mm-hm. So, I'll put this in dramatic play."

Ivory walked over to the dramatic play center to show the children where to find the new activity. I was struck by the manner in which she mimicked all my actions.

"If you need me, I'll be here, okay?" She ended her lesson, and the children began to choose their work.

With sweet tears burning my eyes, I was touched beyond words at what had unfolded before me. At that moment, I understood the gravity of my role as teacher. My every action, movement, and word had been emulated by this young girl. She had even copied the nuances of my speech patterns. Even when I thought that she had shut me out, she had been taking in all that I had said and done. I have always tried to make my words and actions as respectful as possible for all of my students. I now understood the true importance of my efforts. As teachers, we are some of the closest role models that children have. For a little girl, who had been beaten so badly that being a scratching, speechless cat was the safest persona to adopt, my words and actions provided Ivory with part of a new foundation for an emerging voice of her own.

A couple of weeks after Ivory's alligator-crocodile lesson, Marc spoke to Ivory as if she was a cat. She quickly and matter-of-factly stated, "I'm not a cat anymore. No. I'm not a cat. Not anymore." Her round face was soft. Her almond-shaped eyes were clear. Through the support and understanding of her peers, her claws and teeth had transformed into the gentle hands and soft mouth of a little girl.

Today, Ivory is a poised third grader. Ivory's healing did not happen in the sterile vacuum of a test-frenzied institution, but rather within the loving walls of a child-centered school. Ivory's traumatic experience had been met with compassion and healing at our school, but I am concerned for the multitude of Ivorys within the overstandardized schools throughout our nation. So many young children who have experienced severe trauma are met with stony cold curricula, as the trend toward testing in the younger grades drastically increases.

Studies of preschool and kindergarten-aged children indicate that social and emotional skills are better predictors of success and satisfaction in later life than are academic skills.[1] When the curriculum focuses exclusively on meeting academic standards—without adequate attention to the social curriculum and its relevance to children's lives—children like Ivory suffer. Standardized tests and benchmark targets are a distraction from the real lessons that children need to rise above adversity and succeed in life.

In this age of standardized testing, I consider myself fortunate to work under the leadership and guidance of a principal, Aviva Kafka, who recognizes the transcending purpose of schools to heal and transform lives. Aviva was honored recently with an award for excellence in administration. She told me that this distinction had come at a good time, as she had been feeling discouraged that our school's test scores had plateaued after a few years of steady climbing. I realized for the first time that as building administrator, she was affected by testing targets far more than I was. Principals face significant demands to improve their test scores or face dire punitive action, including having funds cut and being forced to implement a highly scripted, stand-and-deliver curriculum. Yet, Aviva had successfully shielded her staff from these concerns, as neither her actions nor her policies indicated that she had felt such pressure. Courageously, she always encouraged her staff to implement practices that were best for young children, not just those that were best for raising test scores. Had I not had the encouragement and support from my principal and other colleagues, I would have likely succumbed to benchmark demands, rather than address the holistic, developmental needs of the students. The outcome of Ivory's kindergarten experience would have been drastically different.

Every year, at least one child like Ivory becomes a part of our class, a child who has experienced more pain than any child should ever encounter. Had my principal forced me to conform to rigid benchmark targets, at the exclusion of the curriculum that springs forth from the children, Ivory would have been denied the opportunity to heal and learn during a critical period in her life. The result could easily have been devastating not only for her education but for her long-term well-being and survival. Additionally, her peers and I would have missed an equally important opportunity to honor and participate in her healing process. As educators, we must dedicate our actions to our highest purpose: honoring and supporting the children who enter our schools.

Having taught kindergarten at Violet Avenue Elementary School in the Hyde Park Central School District in Poughkeepsie, New York, for seven years, Felipa Gaudet currently teaches three- to six-year-olds in the Children's House at George Washington Public Montessori School in the Kingston City School District in Kingston, New York.

Note

1.   Daniel Goleman, *Emotional Intelligence: Why It Can Matter More Than IQ* (New York: Bantam Press, 1997).

15.   You Can't Be Driven by Fear: A Portrait of Public School 24

Tom Roderick

P.S. 24's intimate auditorium is bursting with children, parents, and staff eager to witness the culmination of the fifth graders' work with a resident artist who has been teaching them Mexican dance. Carlos, a painfully shy fifth grader, appears on stage in his wheelchair, dressed in costume, to explain what they will see. As the dancing unfolds before the delighted audience, Carlos deftly steers his wheelchair to join in the dance. "For the kids I'm sure it didn't seem like anything unusual," reflects Christina Fuentes, P.S. 24's principal. "But for the adults, it was a very special moment."

Fuentes recalls this story to explain why the arts are an essential part of the curriculum at P.S. 24. "We're trying to provide an excellent education, and understanding the arts is the mark of a well-educated person. The arts provide entry points for kids who may not be academically oriented. They are also a way to express culture." Every year, Fuentes finds money in her budget to ensure that every class works with a teaching artist.

It might have been otherwise. In 2002, P.S. 24 was labeled a school in need of improvement (SINI) under the No Child Left Behind Act (NCLB). Many school leaders have responded to the SINI stigma by making test prep their top priority.

Not Fuentes. "We do our best to prepare students for the tests," she explains. "It would be irresponsible not to. But we want them to have what we would want for our own children: teachers who are professionals and scholars, learning as well as teaching; a rich curriculum that integrates learning across the disciplines; social studies, science, the arts, and social and emotional learning."

Fuentes and her staff are resisting oppressive federal high-stakes testing mandates and creating a great school—against the odds.

Located in the largely Latino/a, working-class neighborhood of Sunset Park in Brooklyn, P.S. 24 (the Dual Language School for International Studies) has 770 students, grades pre-K–5, half of whom are English-language learners. Most of the children's families have emigrated from Mexico, the Dominican Republic, and other Latin American countries. Almost all of the students are from low-income families, with 95 percent eligible for educational services under Title I. Twenty-one percent are entitled to special education services.

The opening of P.S. 24 in 1997 was a victory for the community. During the early 1990s, Yvette Aguirre, then principal of another school, had led a campaign for a new school to relieve serious overcrowding in the neighborhood's schools. Aguirre became P.S. 24's principal, and a year later Fuentes joined her, first as literacy coach and then as assistant principal. When Aguirre retired in 2004, Fuentes took over.

Fuentes, who grew up in a socially conscious family, with a Puerto Rican father, a mother of Irish and German ancestry, and three siblings, agrees with the stated goal of NCLB and other education reforms to improve education for all children, including those often "left behind"—students of color, students with disabilities, English-language learners, and students from low-income families. But she believes that the all-or-nothing approach of standardized testing is wrong. "These tests use just one measure of student achievement, and that method is deeply flawed," she explains. "The class and cultural bias in the tests is well documented. Many other ways to assess children's progress give a broader and more accurate view."

Furthermore, punitive policies—labeling schools as failing and threatening them with restructuring if students' test scores don't improve—too often produce the opposite of their intended effect. Fuentes observes, "Instead of motivating a school to educate all children, there's a disincentive to have certain kinds of children in the school at all. If a child is struggling and doesn't make adequate progress as defined by federally mandated tests, your school's rating will go down. Some principals find ways to keep the number of kids like this in their schools to a minimum."

Then there's the implicit assumption that closing the achievement gap is solely the school's responsibility. "Real inequities in health services and job opportunities affect children's lives," says Fuentes. "Schools can't fix these injustices, but they get blamed for things that are the consequence of larger social and political problems." She sees the current situation as "almost like a setup to demonstrate that public schools are no good" so that private companies can come to the rescue. Fuentes believes that educators have the responsibility to provide an excellent education for all students, but she wants the rest of society to do its part.

Fuentes would also like government policy to address what Jonathan Kozol called "savage inequalities." Like many schools in low-income communities, P.S. 24 has historically been underfunded. "On top of that," she adds, "the extensive testing program is an unfunded mandate. An enormous amount of staff time goes into administering the tests—resources better spent on enrichments."

Winning competitive grants has helped. A federal Comprehensive School Reform grant enabled P.S. 24 to create its model Dual Language Program. Partnerships with nonprofits contribute resources as well. The school works with Morningside Center for Teaching Social Responsibility to implement its PAZ After-School Program and its innovative activities to foster social and emotional learning. But none of this comes easy. Chasing grants takes lots of extra work, and all schools should have access to resources such as these, not only the few that win grant competitions.

When Fuentes and Aguirre received word in 2002 that P.S. 24 was now a school in need of improvement, they took the news in stride. "We felt it was an inaccurate judgment of the quality of the school," Fuentes recalls. They were determined not to dumb down the curriculum by turning the school into a test-taking factory, but to keep doing what they'd been doing all along: providing a vibrant curriculum that includes the arts, dual-language instruction, and social and emotional learning; running the PAZ After-School Program; involving parents; using data from a variety of sources to improve instruction;

and, yes, preparing students for the tests as best they could—without compromising their vision. They also maintained their commitment to building a professional learning community, inspiring teachers to get excited about ideas and engage in ongoing questioning and reflecting. Fuentes explains, "Professional development takes the form of yearly faculty retreats, summer institutes, working with consultants and in-house coaches, twice-monthly grade conferences, and teacher study groups on topics of their choosing."

As the Dual Language School for International Studies, P.S. 24 offers children the opportunity to learn a second language while developing their first. Half of the school's classes are dual language, with half of the children in those classes Spanish proficient and half English proficient. "Having two languages is a great asset in getting a job," observes former assistant principal, Mariana Gaston. "And validating the child's dominant language builds self-confidence." Social and emotional learning is another priority—for all students. "If we want kids to be risk takers intellectually, we need to help them feel safe," insists Fuentes. "The more we address emotional needs, the fewer discipline problems we have. We're giving students skills for success in life and participation in a democratic society. It's the right thing to do morally, and it helps kids academically."

Since opening its doors in 1997, P.S. 24 has been working with Morningside Center to develop effective approaches for fostering social and emotional learning. The school has become a national model, integrating social and emotional learning into its culture and curriculum and developing innovative practices. Through classroom instruction in Morningside Center's 4Rs program (reading, writing, respect, and resolution), children increase their capacity to understand and manage feelings, relate well to others, make good decisions, deal well with conflict, and take responsibility for improving their communities. Ninety-five students, grades three through five, trained as peer mediators, help their peers talk about conflicts in P.S. 24's cafeteria, playground, and classrooms. "Peace Helpers," the brainchild of a former second grader, create corners in K–2 classes where students who are upset or in conflict can go to calm down, read, think, and perhaps discuss their situation, and a Lunch Club program supports children who need extra help in managing their feelings and behavior.

Another powerful innovation, the student diversity panel, has taken the school's focus on diversity to a new level. A panel typically includes five students representing various forms of diversity who briefly describe mistreatment they've experienced and how they responded. They ask if children in the class have had similar experiences and lead a discussion of how students can make their school a place where such hurtful incidents don't occur because people stand up for themselves and others in a constructive manner. "The impact of the panels has been profound," says Gaston. "The kids' stories are heart-wrenching, but sharing them is a first step toward awareness and healing."

The focus on social and emotional learning doesn't stop when the school day ends. PAZ (Peace from A to Z), the school's award-winning after-school program, serves some 250 children every school day with a rich program of conflict resolution, cooperative games and sports, arts education, community service, and homework help.

When leading the campaign for a new school in Sunset Park, Yvette Aguirre envisioned a place that would be a resource for the entire community. Accordingly, the school is often open on evenings and weekends and hosts community events. But the priority has been to engage parents in the life of the school. Staff members go out of their way to make parents feel welcome; there's always someone available who speaks the parent's language, whether Spanish, Chinese, or Arabic; the school safety agent who signs in visitors is gracious and friendly; and a comfortable, well-provisioned parents' room provides space for meetings and projects. Meetings on such topics as parenting and health are well attended, and parents play a key role on the active and influential school leadership team. "A high point was the year we created the diversity anthology," recalls Gaston. "Parents wrote stories about times they had stood up for themselves and others. We put the stories together in a book we distributed to the school community."

Fuentes views the extensive program of standardized testing imposed by city, state, and federal authorities as a thief stealing time from activities that truly contribute to children's education. But she is hardly anti-data. In fact, she believes in using data to improve instruction, provided it comes from a variety of sources. By examining data, for example, she saw that many students not labeled English-language learners still needed support learning English, and she worked to infuse enriched language development and ESL practices into teaching across the disciplines.

Fuentes doesn't pressure her teachers to do test prep, but they feel the pressure anyway. "I want my students to be prepared and do their best, but after too much test prep, they begin not to care, despite how creative I've tried to make it," says Rachel Bingman, a fourth-grade special education teacher. "My students make progress in baby steps, but who would know that by looking at test scores? What do those numbers represent? Not my students—and not their learning in my classroom."

Teacher Shirley Guerrero adds that the standardized testing program is especially unfair for English language learners—about half of P.S. 24's students. "Research shows that it takes English-language learners five to seven years to achieve academic proficiency," explains Guerrero. "But students have to take the English Language Arts exam after only a year of being registered in a school in the United States."

Part of Fuentes' job description is turning potential setbacks into opportunities. One such "opportunity" came in the spring of 2007 when the New York City Department of Education announced that, in addition to all of the other tests kids were taking, schools would be required to administer "periodic assessment tests" (four each year in reading, four in math, and four for English-language learners). The stated aim of these periodic assessments: to give teachers data on students' strengths and weaknesses so that they can better target instruction.

To their credit, Department of Education officials said they would be open to alternative plans for assessing student progress. So P.S. 24 joined a network of two dozen other schools and two university partners to create another approach. It took lots of meetings—of the entire network, of subcommittees, of Fuentes with her teachers—but the Department of Education approved the network's alternative. "I don't consider standardized exams when grouping my students or guiding my instruction, because they are not a true reflection of student capabilities," says Shirley Guerrero. "I use student portfolios, running records, and informal observations to assess my students—methods that more accurately track student learning and are available immediately."

The clear vision and hard work of Fuentes, her staff, and her non-profit partners are paying off. P.S. 24 is a model for dual-language instruction and for social and emotional learning. Visitors come from near and far to learn from the school's practices. The New York City Department of Education acknowledges the school's excellence by consistently giving the school highest ratings on its annual quality reviews.

But according to NCLB, P.S. 24 has achieved its "adequate yearly progress" (AYP) only once since the law went into effect. One year, the school came within a hair of meeting its AYP but fell short because the families of two special education students, whom the school had nurtured for years, moved out of the school's district and thus their progress could no longer be credited to P.S. 24, even though the students continued to attend the school.

What's wrong with this picture? When a school like P.S. 24 consistently fails to achieve its AYP, one has to question the fairness of a so-called federal education "reform" that judges a school on test score results rather than by authentic, multiple measures of student learning. One also has to question the purpose of the SINI label, which gives mayors and superintendents the excuse to close schools and replace them with charter schools.

Christina Fuentes offers these thoughts to the thousands of educators throughout the country who labor day in and day out to put children first—despite mandated high-stakes tests:

> You can't be driven by fear. You have to be confident of where you're going, have a clear vision, and keep your eyes on that prize. You can't sneak around. You can't do this job scared. There's always the danger of losing your job. But if your decisions are truly based on what is best for students, you can sleep well at night. I'm not going to compromise my deepest convictions. Those convictions are why I do what I do. They're what keep me going.

Tom Roderick is executive director of Morningside Center for Teaching Social Responsibility, based in New York City.

Part IV

Introduction: "Not My Voice Alone"— Organizing to Reclaim Public Education

Injustice can outrage us so much that we are catalyzed into action. And collective action can be far more effective than individualized attempts. In the process of working cooperatively with others, we form bonds, make friends, and learn lessons; regardless of the outcome, we can find meaning and new energy in the struggle itself.

This piece features the voices of those who have engaged in collective, public forms of resistance to reclaim a sense of urgency in fighting for public education. We hear from those who have a vision of what public education can be and how other forms of accountability can replace an overreliance on test scores. Linking vision and strategy, these voices offer compelling examples of ways to act together for progressive, multicultural, democratic schools.

The teachers who write in this section not only have resisted through meaningful classroom pedagogy, but have organized with others to challenge the system that creates the constraints they face in their classrooms. They teach within the system and, at the same time, work to transform it.

Some teachers in this section organized in a single school; others, across a district. We also hear from parents whose collective resistance and action developed into long-standing, influential parent organizations. We learn from these stories that we can envision alternatives to the status quo and realize that our actions are part of a long struggle to maintain democratic, public education.

The stories you will read span a decade of collective resistance to neoliberal educational policies. Some stories tell of early resistance to high-stakes testing agendas, which have since become pervasive. More recent stories tell of resistance to mayoral control, school closings and turnarounds, charter schools, merit pay, and school resegregation.

While some of the organizing efforts met immediate goals, and others were less successful, they all contributed to the long-range goal of building a movement to fight for more democratic schools. Resisters became empowered, organizations were built, and coalitions were formed. Since we never know how much worse things could have become had people *not* organized, all the narratives validate the importance of taking action. The actions of the resisters here are models of what can be done. They provide inspiration for others who can become part of a critical mass to create the probability of change.

Individual schools can be initial sites of collective resistance, as the first two pieces in this section of the book make clear. Sam Coleman and Edwin Mayorga describe the way Sam organized in his school to defeat a merit-pay system proposed by the New York City school district. Sam and Edwin raise questions for other educators to consider. They argue that bringing school professionals together to engage in a meaningful discussion of policy issues is a democratic practice that should be happening in all schools. The piece also encourages us to ask how educators can help their peers see the importance of the "big picture"—in this case, how a merit-pay plan enhanced a business model of public education.

What began as a lunchroom conversation between Katie Hogan and her colleagues in a Chicago high school became a collective action to protest a counterproductive Chicago test. Katie and eleven other teachers, "the Curie 12," put their careers and livelihoods on the line and signed a letter saying they weren't going to give the test. Katie reflects, "No job is worth having if it comes at the price of checking your beliefs at the door. If teachers are not willing to stand up for their students, who will?" We are inspired to think about how teachers can communicate with colleagues to stand up collectively for the students in their schools.

Entire school districts have been the sites of organized resistance to neoliberal policies by both educators and broader coalitions of concerned people. Some teachers have worked *within* their unions to push to create social justice unionism. The priorities of unions with a social justice agenda include building alliances with parents and communities, actively involving teachers in running the union, promoting antiracist and social justice curricula, and organizing members to fight for social justice in all areas of society.

Principles of social justice unionism are at work in Bob Peterson's heartening story of resistance to the proposed mayoral takeover of the Milwaukee Public Schools. This effort focused on building a coalition of twenty-eight diverse organizations that put aside other differences to work together against incredible odds in order to keep school governance community-based. Bob urges teacher unions to be guided by a social justice perspective and become involved in struggles that are not directly related to school issues, so that the basis for coalitions is always present.

Among the most creative resisters have been parent organizations. According to parent organizer Juanita Doyon, "Parents are the final line of defense against harmful educational policy. Parents have the right and responsibility to protect their children from irresponsible, invalid, unproven practice." Juanita is like many parents who became activists because they saw the impact of high-stakes testing and other market-driven policies on their children. She organized Mothers Against WASL [Washington Assessment of Student Learning], holding "street-corner rallies" to share information with other parents about how to have their children opt out of the tests. Taking on "grocery line activism," Mothers Against WASL made thirty thousand two-and-a-half-inch antitesting buttons with wording like "My Child Is Not Your Data," and distributed them locally and nationally. As Juanita reminds us, "Resistance on the part of parents is never futile. In fact, just saying no is the only sure thing. What if they gave the test and nobody came?"

Chicago was home to Arne Duncan's school reform program, a model for the Race to the Top initiative. It is also the home of PURE, Parents United for Responsible Education, whose advocacy and research have called into question how successful the Duncan program, which closed sixty schools and created one hundred new charter schools, really was. Julie Woestehoff tells the story of how PURE educated parents to fight against high-stakes testing, school closings, and the imposition of a business model on education that justified attempts to break teacher unions and privatize schools. One of PURE's keys to success in organizing parents is its series of fact and tip sheets, with topics such as "Charter School Myths" or "Myths about Turnaround Schools." These and other excellent additional fact sheets from FairTest, the National Center for Fair and Open Testing, are found on the *Educational Courage* website (www.beacon .org/educationalcourage).

"For us to subject children to this one-dimensional, high-stakes testing regime is nothing short of educational malpractice. Therefore I must respectfully decline to administer the test," wrote middle school teacher Don Perl. This act of civil disobedience ultimately led to the creation of the Coalition for Better Education, a Colorado organization that for ten years has been organizing against high-stakes testing and other neoliberal educational policies. Its advertising campaigns on park benches and billboards show parents how they can opt their children out of the Colorado tests. Don reminds educators, parents, and concerned citizens that "what we do locally is of critical importance. The lessons in critical thought, courage, and commitment that we leave our children, and the support we offer their parents, can have positive results beyond our imaginings."

Parent organizers from New York City describe several campaigns to preserve public education and the strategies that made them effective. Jane Hirschmann shares how the group Time Out From Testing fought to maintain portfolio assessments, an evaluation used in lieu of high-stakes tests in some city high schools. Also undermining public education is the resegregation of city schools, often accompanying a community's gentrification. Ujju Aggarwal and Donna Nevel describe the work of the Center for Immigrant Families, a collectively run organization of low-income women of color. They organized to fight the creation of segregated enclaves that allowed for the establishment of pseudo-private schools in the public school system that typically kept out immigrant students. Through their organized efforts, "a community regained its own sense of power and strength—something that can't be undone."

The final narratives in this part of *Educational Courage* point us toward the future. They provide an alternative vision of what public education can be and offer wisdom about ways to move ahead. Chris Gallagher and Doug Christensen use educator and organizer Miles Horton's image of "the long haul" to guide us forward. They write, "Horton knew democracy is a long-term project. So he devoted his life to the patient pursuit of democratic education, trusting that '[w]hat people need are experiences in democracy, in making democratic decisions that affect their lives and communities.'" Writers in this book and all those across the country who have taken steps to resist the ambush of public education are participants in the long haul toward democratic education. Horton, Gallagher, and Christensen give us critical advice: "Rely on your vision, your hope, your resolve. You will need them—*we all will need them*—for the long haul."

"Voices of Activism" contains accounts of people acting collectively and linking the struggle to reclaim public education to other struggles for a more democratic society. Raza Program alumna Kim Dominguez describes why she was willing to be arrested to challenge legislation barring ethnic studies from Arizona public schools. Sarah Knopp and Gillian Russom point to the importance of social justice unionism as a vehicle for coalition building and effective collective action to regain public schools. Bob Peterson, Stephanie Walters, Kathy Xiong, and Brian Jones describe the energy and power of large demonstrations that bring allies together to speak truth to power when public schools, and many other public institutions, are threatened. These varied voices and actions reflect the rallying cry of these larger public protests—"This is what democracy looks like."

Bill Ayers challenges us to choose hope: "Hope is an antidote to cynicism and despair. . . . Hopefulness holds out the possibility of change." He proposes transforming our schools to provide young people with opportunities to exercise their resourcefulness and solve real problems in their communities. Bill urges us to actively create schools as they could be: "We are never freer as teachers and students, citizens, residents, activists, and thinkers than when we refuse to see the situation or the world before us as the absolute end of the matter. Whatever is the case stands side-by-side with what *could* be or *should* be the case. Choose life: choose possibility; choose action."

16.   "You Want to Pay Me for What?!?": Resisting Merit Pay and the Business Model of Education

Sam Coleman and Edwin Mayorga

The story we tell is a single act of resistance within a single public school in New York City. This is a local victory, but we believe that it is a sign that ordinary teachers everywhere are summoning the will to stand up for what is just, fair, and equitable, even as the attacks on our profession, our students, and their families become deeper and more damaging. We hope that local acts of resistance like this one can encourage a few more teachers, and those, a few more, and so on. We start with Sam's story of how he acted to stop the implementation of a merit-pay program at his school. Then we discuss how Sam's act of courage can instruct and inspire others.

Sam's Story

This story starts during my third year as a teacher in a dual-language program (English-Spanish) in a public elementary school in Sunset Park, Brooklyn. From the beginning, there were moments in my daily life as a teacher when I felt uncomfortable with what I was teaching and how I was teaching it. Even as I worked to create and implement a curriculum that engaged my students with the world, through a lens of their own and their families' experiences, I found myself narrowing the curriculum in order to find time to prepare my students for state tests. In order to make up for the fact that most of my students spoke a language other than English at home and were, according to the state, not on grade level for reading, I found that I often had to spend between one and three hours a day teaching my students how to outwit the tests. These were "high-stakes" tests because students needed to pass them in order to be promoted to the next grade, regardless of school performance. Although research shows that it takes five to seven years for English-language learn-ers (ELLs) to develop academic proficiency in their second language, my students were expected to take the same tests that native English speakers take, despite the fact that many of my students had spent only *one* year in an English-speaking environment. I was discovering that our educational system was in fact designed to force teachers to ignore good pedagogy in favor of finding ways to help students pass these tests. So, while there were moments when I saw myself as an agent of change, I would also go home wondering if I was doing more harm than good. My work was a giant contradiction.

As I began to pay more attention to my own practice, and its fluctuation between resistance to and support of the status quo, I also was thinking about the larger policy issues and changes that were swirling around the world of education. I began to make some connections. Nationally, the anti-immigrant policy swing has been coupled with a resistance to bilingual education. Consequently, no consideration was given to the benefits of taking a few extra years to develop bilingual and biliterate children. National and state test-ing requirements were forcing me to teach to tests, a clear disservice to all students, but particularly damaging to our society's most vul-nerable students, including ELLs and students with disabilities. So, as a third-year teacher, with my teacher education coursework and master's degree finally complete, with a feeling of breathing room back in my life, I decided it was time to get involved in combating unjust policies.

An opportunity to act came soon after the school year had be-gun. I had been to a few meetings of New York Collective of Radical Educators (NYCoRE), a local collective of current and former public school educators committed to working for educational justice, but I had not been able to carve out the time needed to engage in political work. This year, I had finally found enough time to get involved. The educational issue that NYCoRE was working on that most resonated for me was the unjust policies regarding testing. I objected to the use of standardized test results/scores to judge the success of schools, principals, teachers, and students when I could clearly see that the tests were unfair. NYCoRE had just restarted Justice Not Just Tests (JNJT), a working group formed to resist the use of standardized and high-stakes tests, so I began going to the meetings. Working on the belief that high-stakes testing was part of a larger agenda for a business model of school reform that was pervasive in our school system, JNJT set out to choose a specific issue to look at and find a way to resist it. It was around this time that the mayor-controlled New York City Department of Education (DOE) proposed to pilot a teacher merit-pay system called the "bonus plan."

New York City's Bonus Plan

Merit-pay plans, simply defined, are pay incentive systems based on individual performance. For educators, merit-pay plans have been primarily based on "student achievement"—a concept that is often equated with test scores. In some cases, school systems have introduced merit pay against the wishes of the local teacher union; in others, with their tacit support; and still others, with their full endorsement. The bonus plan came into the New York City school system by way of a deal our union, the United Federation of Teachers (UFT), made with the DOE during contract negotiations. At the time, neither side spoke about the bonus plan, at least not with us, the rank-and-file teachers.

The contract stated that there was to be a pilot program involving two hundred schools during the first year. The schools chosen served a majority of low-income students of color. These individual schools would vote on whether to accept the merit-pay plan. Approval of the plan required that 55 percent of each school's educators vote in favor of it. If approved, the DOE would set targets for that school's raw test scores and level of improvement over the previous year's scores. Discussions about scores did not involve school staff in any way, despite the fact that the scores would account for 85 percent of the formula for determining a school's eligibility for the bonus. The other 15 percent would come from a formula involving student attendance and the results of parent and teacher surveys on school environment. If the school met the target numbers, it would receive a lump sum of $3,000 per UFT member (50 members = $150,000). A committee made up of the principal, a person selected by the principal, and two UFT members elected by the staff would meet to decide how to distribute the money. The committee could decide to share the money with all staff members; alternatively it could give the money only to those teachers whose students did well or only to those who taught subjects that were tested. If they could not reach a consensus on how to divide the money, it would be forfeited.

The bonus plan brought both a sense of outrage and opportunity for the JNJT work group. We were still gathering information at the time, but we could see that a merit-pay program based on testing would, among many things, divide union members, further narrow the curriculum, and reinforce impoverished notions of "best pedagogical practice" and "student achievement." Tackling the bonus plan also presented a good opportunity for action because there would have to be a vote in every one of the two hundred schools. This meant that instead of having to change the minds of inaccessible DOE officials or lobbying union leadership, JNJT members would be able to appeal directly to colleagues in a common language based on the realities of the classroom. We felt that if we could clearly and concisely express what we felt was wrong with implementing the bonus plan, we would have a chance to convince *at least some schools* to vote against the program. A major hitch, obviously, was that money was involved, and in talking to teachers, we could not forget that this program offered a chance for $3,000 dollars. For many of our colleagues, that money would make a real difference in their personal economic situations. We had to be thoughtful about our approach.

Taking a Stand

The opportunity to put the JNJT plan into practice came much more quickly than we expected. The day after we had decided to make merit pay our target, I found a joint DOE-UFT memo in my box at school announcing that our school had been selected as a site for the bonus plan. The memo came to us on a Thursday morning, and it mandated that we have the vote by the following Wednesday.

That weekend, with the help of JNJT members, I wrote the following leaflet:

12/10/07

Dear Colleagues,

The offer to have our school participate in the merit pay pilot program was thrown at our community without giving us enough time to carefully consider the consequences. I spent the weekend doing some research and here are some thoughts. . . .

I hope everyone can make the meeting on Tuesday to discuss this.

Some Things to Consider Regarding Merit Pay
- The proposed plan implies that the most reliable measure of a school's success is the student's test scores.
- By accepting this plan we are encouraging the use of high-stakes testing and encouraging teachers to teach to the test. (You get money only if students perform well on a test!)
- This plan diverts our attention from the real questions we should be asking our union and our city government: why isn't this money going to reduce class size, increase teacher salaries in general, and increase arts and other enrichment programs.
- This plan creates a situation where the principal, someone the principal designates and two UFT members sit behind closed doors and decide how the money will be divided. This has the potential for some inequitable decisions as well as for creating a divisive atmosphere in our school.
- Merit pay implies that the problem in our schools is that teachers are not working hard enough. "If only those teachers would try a little harder, our students would succeed." It does not address any of the larger issues that we know impact our students' success.
- By accepting merit pay, we are sending the message that we agree with the analysis that teachers are the problem.

- We have to meet 100% of the goal to get the money. (We still do not know how the goals will be set, or who will set them.) If we vote for this plan, and only reach 99% of our goal, we only get 50% of the money ($1,500).
- If we vote for this plan, and reach 74% of our goal, we get nothing.
- With all of the issues to consider and unanswered questions, why are we being rushed to make such a hasty decision?
- Finally, what we do in P.S. 24 will impact what happens in New York City, and what happens in New York sets a precedent for the nation. We have a responsibility to carefully weigh this decision.
- $1,500 is a substantial amount of money. This is a tough decision for everyone. Come to the meeting on Tuesday afternoon so we can figure this out together.

Over the next two days, many of my colleagues came to my classroom or stopped me in the hall to thank me and say that they had not thought about all the implications of merit pay. The following Tuesday, there was a buzz in the school, and by 3:15, forty of the ninety UFT members in the building had gathered in the auditorium to discuss the proposal. There was a palpable anger in the room, and it quickly became clear that most of the people who had come to the meeting were opposed to the bonus plan. As my colleagues got up to speak, it was exciting (especially to someone new to activism) to hear comments such as: "Like Sam said in his letter, they are trying to blame us for the problems in our schools." The next day, we voted. When it was over, the bonus plan had been defeated by a seventy-to-thirty margin. We, as a school, had taken a decisive stand.

After the vote, I posted a report of what had happened on the NYCoRE Listserv (reaching more than 1,500 people) to let people know that my leaflet was available for others to use. I received a lot of congratulations, a number of requests for the leaflet, and some advice about how to deal with this issue in other schools. Since then,

JNJT has been in touch with teachers in other schools that had voted against merit pay, allowing us to build our network as we look to continue the fight against various educational injustices.

Edwin and Sam Reflect on Sam's Act of Courage

There are many lessons we can draw from Sam's act of courage. First, we (the authors) think Sam's story is a wonderful model for change based on a process of reflection, analysis, and action—an approach Brazilian thinker Paolo Freire described as *liberation.*

Sam's act of courage began with his reflection on the injustices that are present in the "trees and forest" of the educational landscape. Merit-pay plans are a wakeup call about the almost silent attack being waged on public education by the business model of school reform. In New York City, the business model is a Hydra that includes mayoral control, marginalized parent and community input, punitive assessment systems, the closing of allegedly failing schools, and the expansion of largely nonunionized and undemocratic charter schools. We acknowledge that public education has been flawed and, in some instances, a failure, particularly for the poor and working class, people of color, those who identify as LGBTQ, ELLs, and students with disabilities. However, we believe that business-model advocates ignore the needs of these populations and overlook the many teachers and schools that have succeeded in the past. Instead they see education as the next "big enchilada"—a part of the public sector that is ripe for acquisition by private industry. Public education is under siege, and the work of public education advocates means both defending public education and demanding systemic change that puts students and teachers at the center.

Sam's story also reminds us to consider the promises and pitfalls of teacher unions. Historically, unions have been central to improving work conditions, and there is a lesser-known history of "social justice unionism" that has brought communities and multiple unions together to make change. Unfortunately, the promise of tackling issues beyond contract bargaining has diminished over time. Antilabor laws hamper the ability of unions (particularly public-sector unions) to organize and strike. Perhaps most frustratingly, unions will sometimes limit their own democratic process in order to appease management, make deals with politicians, and keep particular leaders in power. Still, we remain hopeful, as grassroots organizing by educators in places like Chicago, Milwaukee, Los Angeles, and Washington, DC, have led to the election of more justice-oriented union leaders. We believe that understanding how unions operate and moving them toward social justice unionism will greatly affect the depth of analysis and the power of action by educators.

What should be evident is that acting courageously means traversing complicated terrain, first through careful analysis and then taking well-informed action. Sam and JNJT moved from analyzing the bonus plan and the conditions surrounding it to the transformative act of sharing a simple leaflet—a democratic union practice that we believe should be happening everywhere. Analyses must be shared through conversations, written statements, rallies, and community-made films like *The Inconvenient Truth Behind Waiting for Superman.* By sharing knowledge, people are able to develop language and tools for understanding what troubles them and build their capacity to take action.

"We Must Be in This Together!"

Living and working in tough times, educators are in a vulnerable position, but stories like Sam's raise hope. Sam's story illustrates how powerful and necessary it is to *stand up* and *stand together* for a more just world.

Standing up positively affected Sam's morale and his own personal sense of agency. He was able to negotiate the difficult contradictions of teaching in public schools. Even though Sam found he had to do things that were not instructionally sound to help his students, he was also working for systemic changes that would help all educators and students.

Sam's story also teaches us that we must *stand together.* While this story focuses on one individual, there is no way that Sam would have acted without the support of NYCoRE. Working with others affirms the efforts of the individual and inspires collective activity. Recently, current and retired teachers have organized themselves into groups like the Caucus of Rank-and-File Educators (CORE) in Chicago and Grassroots Education Movement (GEM) in New York City to broaden the voice of educators in communities and to advocate for social justice unionism. Working along with organizations like NYCoRE, we all seek to reclaim democracy within the unions, schools, and communities.

In the end, Sam's act of courage should refuel those of us committed to defending and transforming public education. There are many of us out there in the fight. By working collectively, honing a deeper understanding of what affects education, and taking action, we are creating a groundswell of strength that will help us challenge the daunting situation we all face.

Sam Coleman is a third-grade dual-language teacher and an organizer for educational justice in Brooklyn, New York. Edwin Mayorga, a former public school teacher, is a parent, a PhD candidate at the Graduate Center-City University of New York, and a member of NYCoRE.

17.   The Curie 12: A Case for Teacher Activism

Katie Hogan

"You know, we're all going to be sitting back here in three months grading these damn tests anyways."

That was Mary, getting some nervous laughter out of the group of twelve teachers gathered at the local Polish diner. Just one week earlier, we had sat down in Sara Spachman's living room to write our justification for refusing to give the CASE, or Chicago Academic Standards Examination, to our students at the end of the semester. We had a solid argument against the mandated test, we had data to back us up, and we had the support of our department chair. What we didn't have was any known precedent for what we had just done. Teachers refusing to give a standardized exam mandated by the city? And in Chicago, a city with an education system run by the mayor? Come on. We were tiny bugs waiting to be stepped on. And we knew it. Yet what took place over the course of the last few months of 2002 was not a story of defeat. It wasn't a story of total triumph and transformation either. It was just a simple story, one we might tell later to another colleague at a late-night bar. It started like this . . .

Beginning in 1998, ninth- and tenth-grade core-subject teachers in the Chicago Public Schools were mandated by the city to give an end-of-semester test that supposedly assessed student progress. The idea for this exam was not necessarily a bad one. Systemwide students' scores on national exams like the ACT and SAT were dismal, and there was no common language related to a curriculum to help teachers to ensure quality instruction.

Enter the CASE exam. CASE was supposed to measure student learning according to state standards. Teachers and administrators, the board of education said, could use CASE scores as a means to gauge progress. Sounds good on paper, right? Yet CASE became another beast of standardized testing that measured not student progress, but the already existing inequities of the city's school system. Magnet school students did great. Non-magnet school students did poorly.

After watching my freshmen take the CASE during my first year of teaching at Curie, a three-thousand-student high school on Chicago's southwest side, I felt the disillusionment and disappointment only a rookie teacher can feel. I knew my students were doing their best, and I knew they were all much better readers and writers than they'd been when they walked in my door the first day of class. Still, they had looked at the test questions with confusion and seemed to be panicking as they tried to get through the reading passages. What was going on?

I looked over the test and was shocked. Instead of a skills-based test using the Illinois learning standards, I saw a poorly written, content-based test that asked students seemingly random questions unrelated to the curriculum of survey literature. One question asked students to write an essay explaining the satire of a piece that was not satirical in the least. Who was writing this test? And who was benefiting from it? We had just spent four weeks of instructional time going over the material that was supposed to be on the CASE, and three days of actual test taking. How, I wondered, did this help my students? The answer was that it didn't.

I soon realized that I was not alone in my hatred of the CASE exam. Pretty much every teacher I knew loathed it. But when I asked why no one had done anything about it, I got at most a shrug, or a "you'll understand soon, kid." I was frustrated, angry, and most of all I felt like a fake. I had become a teacher to effect change, and instead I was becoming complicit in maintaining the systems of power that kept my students from achieving their dreams.

I began my second year in the classroom with a very clear desire to start fighting this test. One day in September, another English teacher, Marty McGreal, and I had lunch. After joking around for a bit the conversation turned toward the CASE.

"Why doesn't someone just refuse to give it?" I asked Marty.

"We could," he smiled.

"No, I'm serious. We need some major movement or university to support us."

"It wouldn't be easy. You wouldn't be fighting just CPS, but the mayor's office, as well. Not to mention everyone who profits from this test."

"I just can't give it anymore," I said.

Marty stopped eating and looked at me. "Let's not give it," he said.

"Are you sure? We could be fired."

Marty's eyes flashed cold. "Yes, I'm sure."

From that lunchroom conversation, our "movement" was born. I began mentioning to a few other teachers in the English department that Marty and I weren't going to give the test.

"What do you mean, you're not going to give the test? You have to give it," most responded.

"No, I'm serious. We're not going to give it. We're going to write up a press release with our evidence and send it to Chicago Public Schools and the papers."

The response was not quite as enthusiastic as we had hoped. While a few teachers quickly voiced their support, most looked away and pretended to do other work. And that's the part of this whole thing that I will never understand. Teachers stand up every day and inspire students with their words and presence. They work hours without pay beyond almost every profession. They sacrifice their time, spirits, and energies for the education of youth, yet when it comes to expressing publicly their beliefs about testing, you might as well be talking to a roomful of sheep.

In the end, only ten other teachers—all English teachers except for one social studies teacher—decided to join our protest. I can remember clearly the moment we all signed our names to the paper. It was quiet in Sara's house. We were all scared. Those of us without

tenure feared we could be fired without due process the day this letter hit the papers. For those with tenure, it could clearly be seen as an
act of insubordination and grounds for dismissal. Yet every teacher
in that living room put his or her career and livelihood on the line
that day. We weren't sure what to expect. The only thing we truly
hoped for was a public discussion about the CASE.

The day the letter was received by Chicago Public Schools (CPS)
and hit every major Chicago newspaper, our department was in
chaos. People wanted to talk to the rebel teachers who wouldn't give
the test. They wanted to know if we would handcuff ourselves to the
doors if they tried to drag us out. CPS wanted an immediate meeting
with our principal and those who had sent the letter. Students lined
up by our desks to ask if that was really us in the newspaper and if
we were really risking our jobs for them. My mother wanted to know
if I was going to have to move back home after losing my job. I had
never been so exhilarated.

Three factors clearly helped our claims. First, we had hard data supporting our assertion that the CASE exam did not improve instruction, but instead actually hurt student achievement. Second, we had
let our administration know in advance what we were planning to
do. Third, we elected Marty McGreal and Vera Wallace, two veteran
teachers, as the spokespeople of the group to ensure we could not be
attacked individually.

In the months that followed, we had meeting after meeting
with officials from CPS. They sent the heads of every department
I could imagine over to the school to talk to us. But we refused to
back down. We were prepared to be fired for this cause, so there
was nothing they could threaten us with to which we couldn't say,
"If that's what you need to do, then do it." We were on television,
on the radio, and in local and national papers. Teachers from all
over the country wrote and told us how proud they were. I stood in
front of my students each day with a clear conscience.

"How do you know when to trust someone?" students have asked me.

"When their words and actions match," I would always reply.

For the first time in my short career as a teacher, my words of promoting justice and fighting for rights matched my actions. The twelve of us were not fakes, and the students saw it.

In December, the central office suddenly issued a press release saying that the CASE exams were being discontinued, not just at Curie, but throughout CPS. And not just for the next round of tests, but permanently. In a system of over 600 schools, 26,000 teachers, and 400,000 students, 12 teachers had spoken out in a way that brought about systemwide change.

The new CEO of Chicago's schools at the time, Arne Duncan, never gave credit to any movement to abolish the CASE, but we knew what it had taken. We celebrated at a local bar as we watched Vera and Marty on television responding to our victory. Even the librarian, who was not known for her team spirit, put down $20 for a round for the Curie 12, as we had been dubbed. It was a good day to be a teacher in Chicago.

In the years since the fight to end the CASE, I have been asked to speak or write about my experience frequently. I have always maintained that teacher activism is the essential ingredient for student activism. We were not twelve overly sophisticated intellectuals who wanted to buck the system. We were not twelve angry teachers who wanted to tell CPS to shove it. We were just twelve regular teachers on different ends of the activism spectrum who wanted to end a really bad test. We never expected to win; we only expected to fight. Isn't that what we should teach our students every day?

For me, being a teacher is not a profession: it is my art, my craft, and my life. I want to walk through my life with thoughtfulness and courage. I want my students to see me acting in a manner that befits the sacredness of the profession. And I also want to remember that no job is worth having if it comes at the price of checking your beliefs at the door. If teachers are not willing to stand up for their students, who will?

Katie Hogan is an eleven-year teaching veteran of the Chicago Public Schools.

18. The Struggle against Mayoral Control in Milwaukee

Bob Peterson

It's hard to find reasons for hope in the "education wars" these days—brutal budget cuts, massive testing schemes, and news stories about hedge fund aristocrats funding private charter school franchises. These are enough to make any educator feel powerless.

Probably the last place people would look for a story of hope is in Milwaukee, Wisconsin, a city about sixty miles north of Chicago with a school system of eighty-five thousand mostly black and Latino students. In Milwaukee, school politics have been dominated by privatizing forces for two decades.

And yet, since August 2009, a rather remarkable struggle unfolded in which grassroots organizing stopped the powerful forces of a mayoral takeover of the public schools.

For years, Milwaukee has been ground zero for school privatization efforts. Right-wing foundations and philanthropists like the Bradley Foundation and the Walton Family Foundation have spent millions of dollars to pressure politicians to maintain and expand the United States' largest publicly funded private-school voucher program. The *Wall Street Journal* has editorialized about the school board elections in Milwaukee to promote pro-privatization candidates. The Wisconsin state legislature has seen fit to spend nearly a half-billion dollars for private schools in Milwaukee and yet does nothing to change a grossly unfair public school funding system.

Milwaukee is beset with deep problems, in both the schools and the community. Large sections of the African American community have been suffering depression-like conditions for more than a decade, with jobless rates among black males as high as 55 percent in certain neighborhoods. Milwaukee's rates of childhood poverty, teenage pregnancy, infant mortality, and racial gaps in school achievement rank among the worst in the nation.

In 2008, Wisconsin's Democratic governor and Milwaukee's Democratic mayor hired the international consulting firm McKinsey & Company to evaluate the Milwaukee public schools. With no input from teachers or parents, the firm issued a report outlining ways to save more than $100 million. Proposals including laying off food-service workers (by using prepackaged lunches), increasing from one to fifteen the number of school buildings engineers should be responsible for, and denying full health benefits to part-time employees.

In 2009, the governor and mayor, in an attempt to implement the recommendations, called for a mayoral takeover of the schools and the dismantling of the democratically elected nine-person school board. They received support from U.S. Secretary of Education Arne Duncan.

Initially this proposal seemed like a slam-dunk. Such top-down governance switches are a national trend, promoted by Duncan, who told the Associated Press last spring that he "will have failed" if, when his tenure is up, more urban districts aren't in mayors' hands.

One of the governor and mayor's key arguments was that mayoral control would curry favor with Duncan and almost guarantee that Wisconsin would be selected as a recipient for the Race to the Top funds.

The governor and mayor started to line up support in the state legislature. The daily newspaper hailed the dramatic school improvements in cities where mayors have replaced elected school boards.

We activists started to organize. Within a few weeks, Educators' Network for Social Justice—a network of public school and college teachers—and the local NAACP put together a coalition. Over time, the Coalition to Stop the MPS Takeover grew to twenty-eight organizations, including locals from the American Federation of Teachers and the National Education Association and many individual activists.

Meeting weekly at the NAACP office, teachers, parents, neighborhood association members, church pastors, community and union activists, students, and a few politicians debated direct action tactics and lobbying strategies. Meetings were at times contentious, as the coalition brought together organizations that had serious past differences. From the first meeting, members agreed that significant changes had to be made to improve the schools, but that changes in governance wasn't one of them.

Members of the African American and Latino communities viewed the matter as a question of basic democracy. "We have struggled for over one hundred years to protect and sustain our right to vote," explained Jerry Ann Hamilton, president of the Milwaukee branch of the NAACP, "and we are not going to allow our rights to be taken away from us now."

Ultimately, the coalition united on three things: oppose the mayoral takeover, protect and defend voter rights, and invest in parent and community involvement in our schools.

The coalition organized rallies at city hall, attended public forums on the issue, and held press conferences. Members distributed thousands of flyers and appeared on local radio and TV shows. When the mainstream media failed to cover our activities, we borrowed a tactic from the civil rights movement and picketed the homes of the two Milwaukee legislators who sponsored the mayoral control legislation. The spirited picket lines further energized coalition members.

It was an uphill battle. The coalition was up against not only the powerful Democratic governor and mayor, but other forces as well. The *Milwaukee Journal Sentinel,* which is anti–teacher union and has supported the expansion of the voucher program, editorially endorsed mayoral control, labeling those who oppose it "defenders of the status quo." The paper also refused to report on any of the coalition's press conferences or activities or even mention the coalition's name in any print news article.

Nationally, Democrats for Education Reform (DFER) and Education Reform Now (ERN), based in New York City, intervened through their Wisconsin staff. Those two groups, whose boards of directors include major financial investors and supporters of private charter schools, have been pushing the Democratic Party to support market-based reforms in education.

Part of the coalition's strategy was educational. We created a blog and used Facebook and e-mail as key ways to communicate. We hosted a public event of Chicago union activists who detailed the negative consequences of mayoral control and Duncan's time as superintendent. We used *Rethinking Schools* magazine, which is based in Milwaukee, and worked closely with both the Milwaukee Teachers' Education Association and our statewide affiliate, the Wisconsin Education Association Council. We ran articles and editorials about the dangers of mayor control and the campaign in Milwaukee to stop it.

Despite the efforts of the media, the business community, and their political operatives, the pro-mayoral control forces were unable to out-organize us. A culminating event was a January hearing in front of the State Senate Education Committee. During the eleven-hour hearing, in which some members of the public had to wait six hours to testify, "No Takeover" signs and buttons dominated the hall. The sentiment was overwhelmingly opposed, with eighty-one speakers against and only twenty in favor. This fact didn't stop the *Milwaukee Journal Sentinel* from reporting the following day that "members of the public at the hearing were fairly evenly divided."

By the end of January, the Wisconsin legislature voted to close its special session that had been convened by the governor to push mayoral control. While the governor refused to admit defeat, leading legislators announced the plan was "dead."

What can we learn from the coalition's success? A key component of that success was the patient organizing and coalition building that are at times neglected when activists focus mainly on large mobilizations. Public demonstrations were an important ingredient of the Milwaukee experience, but building relationships and focusing on a deep understanding of the issues laid the foundation. Those relationships are built over time; in this case, some had been forged two years earlier when community and educators' groups had mounted a successful campaign against the adoption of a racist and antiworker social studies elementary textbook series.

If teacher unions only seek to build coalitions when our self-interests are threatened, our capacity to build such coalitions is compromised. We need to be guided by a social justice perspective and be involved in struggles that are not directly related to school issues. Moreover, unions should encourage their members to teach about social justice issues. It's important for two reasons: first, it educates the students—future members of society—on how to be active, critical participants in our society. Second, it politically educates the teachers. It will change attitudes of teachers. In the United States, too many teachers don't know the real peoples' history of our nation—they don't learn it in the teacher training courses—whether it's the heroic resistance of native peoples, the working-class struggles, the work of women's rights activists, the movements for civil rights, or the struggle against U.S. imperialism. The more successful we are in promoting social justice education among our members, the greater will be their capacity and willingness to be active in our political campaigns.

Even more basic to the success in Milwaukee was the simple, yet often elusive recognition that, even in difficult times, believing that people can change reality is essential.

As the late Howard Zinn wrote, "Everything in history, once it has happened, looks as if it had to happen exactly that way. We can't imagine any other. But I am convinced of the uncertainty of history, of the possibility of surprise, of the importance of human action in changing what looks unchangeable."[1]

The success of the Coalition to Stop the MPS Takeover can be a lesson for all of us. We, the people, can shape our futures. We must.

Bob Peterson, president of the Milwaukee Teachers' Education Association, is a thirty-year elementary school teacher in the Milwaukee Public Schools and a founder of Rethinking Schools and La Escuela Fratney.

Note

1. Howard Zinn, *You Can't Be Neutral on a Moving Train* (Boston: Beacon Press, 1994), 101.

19. We Are Not the Backlash: We Are the Resistance!

Juanita Doyon

Don't drink the tea; don't ride the bus; don't take the test. When people tell me there is no hope for ridding the education world of high-stakes testing because the tests are here to stay, I smile and give them my standardized response, "Yes, and women can't vote and drinking fountains are segregated."

It all began with a couple of failing marks on my daughter's Washington Assessment of Student Learning (WASL) scorecard that arrived in the mail in the fall of 1998. Her twin brother had one failing mark, but that was on a dubious test section called "Listening." I hardly needed a state test to break the news that my nine-year-old son could perform better in all other subjects.

Soon after the arrival of failing scores for my academically average to above-average, two-parented, school-respecting fourth graders, I wrote a lengthy e-mail to Washington's State Superintendent of Public Instruction. I asked how my overcrowded school district was supposed to gain support for ballot issues to build new schools, when all this bad test-score news was being blasted across the front page of the local paper and arriving home like so many letter bombs. When I received a condescending reply from the state superintendent's office, I knew the fight was on. Little did I realize I would spend the next ten years and beyond living and protesting on what one school board member labeled "the bleeding edge of reform."

Thank the good Lord for my emerging Internet skills! "High-stakes testing," I Googled. I got out the huge three-ring binder my district had provided during the latest round of facilities meetings, removed pages of enrollment statistics and state-funding formulas, and refilled it. In the clear cover flap, I inserted a graphic of an angry pink rabbit with the caption, "Hot Cross Bunny!" This fight was going to be long and hard, and I would begin with a sense of humor or burn out before my time. I had gained a reputation in my own school district for taking stands where needed, but I knew—or soon found out—that what I was now taking on was not only a state-level battle but a national civil war to take back our schools.

In-State Buddies and National Allies

The Internet is truly the activist's friend. After reading a letter to the editor in my local paper, I located and e-mailed its author, professor emeritus Donald Orlich at Washington State University. Dr. Orlich, who had studied the WASL extensively and accurately predicted that 60 percent of the state's fourth graders would fail the math section, became my first ally in what I soon dubbed the "WASL War." He referred me to a Listserv operated by a candidate for state superintendent. There I found many individuals who shared my aversion to the state test.

Another mother and I began standing on busy street corners with our children, holding big signs with a red-slashed "WASL" and "Honk, No WASL!" We were "Mothers Against WASL" and declared we would never again allow our children to take the state test. We situated our corner rallies at intersections where people could pull over and join us or pick up information, buttons to wear and share, and preprinted forms to "just opt out" of the test.

In-state activity broadened to national activism when someone recommended that I join the Assessment Reform Network (ARN), FairTest's Listserv of parents, teachers, professors, and researchers discussing K–12 testing issues. FairTest is the national nonprofit organization for "fair and open testing." Its website shares a wealth of information, including research and educated opinion. I soon signed on to be the Washington State coordinator for ARN, a volunteer contact for anyone looking for information on testing issues.

I also signed on as the unofficial "button queen of the resistance." Starting with a few red-slashed "WASL" buttons, I was soon designing and making buttons protesting high-stakes tests in other states and harmful education policy in general. The buttons became icebreakers at conferences, where my allies and I would take large plastic bags of assorted buttons for people to choose from. In the first two years of button production, approximately thirty thousand were mailed, handed out, and passed to people who were hungry for our message. With contact information on the back, the buttons also acted as business cards. Pictures of the buttons illustrated articles in education journals. There were so many important things to say that could fit on a two-and-a-half-inch circle: "No Child Left Behind—Drag them all through the misery!" "Choose the best answer: a. teach; b. test." "Kindergarten is not boot camp." "My child is not your data!"

Through ARN, I found many strong, well-informed individuals. I began working closely with Susan Ohanian from Vermont, Carol Holst from Texas, George Schmidt from Illinois, Bill Cala from New York, Don Perl from Colorado, and several other leaders of the test resistance. My knowledge of nationwide education issues increased exponentially.

Just after Washington's state superintendent won reelection, in 2000, I established a goal to unseat her in 2004 and became a candidate for the Office of Superintendent of Public Instruction on what I called "the Parent Ticket." Lacking degrees and certificates, I nevertheless had the advantage of many years' experience as a public school parent and would further my credentials by association with teachers, professors, and researchers, and with acute knowledge of the issues and the office. I began traveling the state and country, meeting in person with the people I had "met" online and attending and presenting at education conferences. All the while, Mothers Against WASL grew as a grassroots force.

The Media Advantage

The war on testing is a war of words. The powers that be have money for all the propaganda their very little hearts desire. They know how to name a corporate nonprofit to sound like an education organization (for instance, Education Trust and Achieve). And they know how to name harmful education policy to sound necessary and progressive (No Child Left Behind, Race to the Top). The trick for us "little guys" with truth on our side is to find ingenious ways to spread the word without breaking the bank. Part of the trick is learning how to use media to our best advantage. The good news is reporters are always looking for the alternate view. The bad news is the alternate view is often trivialized with words like "backlash."

There are several ways to get messages of resistance dispersed through major media. Strategies that work include:

- Letters to the editor—Check your local newspaper's website for guidelines and word limits and stick to them. Smaller papers publish the same writer as often as once per month. Big-city papers may limit writers to once per quarter. Word limits range from 150 to 300. Longer op-ed pieces are approximately 600 words. If you have a title (teacher, parent, organization director, and so on), use it in your signature byline.
- Press releases—Take a stand, lead a protest, and let the media know about it. Develop an e-mail list of local education writers and reporters. Most TV and radio stations depend partly on listeners and viewers to provide news, and most are receptive to press releases that provide "breaking education news" with details and contacts who are willing to be interviewed. With a nonprofit organization behind me, I have sent successful press releases regarding testing errors, protests at the state capital, a teacher refusing to administer the state test, responses to statements made by officials, an illegal student survey attached to the state test, and a possible lawsuit against the state for mandating the state test as a graduation requirement. These press releases, and others, have brought multiple interviews by TV, radio, and newspaper reporters. Several have also resulted in longer radio and TV talk show opportunities. The beauty? No cost, save possible travel expenses to TV or radio studios.

Parent Empowerment Network

When the final score in the primary election of 2004 did not add up to my success, it was time to regroup with my supporters. The campaign for statewide office had served as an effective conduit for our message by providing multiple opportunities for speaking, debating, interviewing, and tabling. Now, we needed a new, official entity from which to present our views.

Mothers Against WASL became a project of a newly formed nonprofit organization, Parent Empowerment Network (PEN), and I worked with my campaign manager and committee to file nonprofit paperwork with the IRS and state. PEN began by paying close attention to education issues at the state and national levels. Through research and strategic communication, we stopped an illegal survey attached to the test; forced the state to follow federal mandates and allow parents to see the test once their children took it; and alerted the media to an offensive, discriminatory test item. Most importantly, we provided information and assistance to parents, teachers, and students struggling in the milieu of high-stakes testing.

The Only Sure Thing—Just Say No!

Throughout my tenure as an education activist, I have carried two important philosophies:

- Never be disappointed by a small turnout or response.
- Parents are responsible for the education of their children.

These are my laws of self-preservation, and they remind me that I cannot take responsibility for the actions of others or all the troubles of the education world.

As I've counseled parents about the state test and their parental rights, I've encouraged them to decide for themselves whether or not their child should take the test. In Washington, as in many other states, parents have the right to refuse state testing of their children. Parents who understand that their children do not belong to the state, and that schools do not have the right to dictate all aspects of the educational program, are better able to navigate the system and assert themselves as the final say when it comes to assessment and placement.

In order for schools to provide a Free and Appropriate Public Education (FAPE) for every student (as mandated by federal law), teachers and parents must work together, and parents must understand the system well enough to advocate for their children. The only way to ensure that students do not suffer negative consequences from taking the state test or from scores received on the state test, is for parents to refuse to allow the state to test their children. This becomes more difficult when the test is required for high school graduation, but often alternatives can be found through careful study of laws and policies.

Just before my twins began their seventh-grade year, I asserted myself as the final say in their education by sending the following letter to editors of area newspapers:

> My two seventh graders will not take WASL (Washington Assessment of Student Learning) tests next spring. It is my right as their parent to keep them home during testing week. I believe WASL tests are harmful to our schools, our communities and our children.
>
> Public education in our state is slipping further from the real world of parents, children and communities. The success of public schools has long been based on local support and control. If public schools are to meet societal challenges, they must be free to assess themselves locally and request state assistance when it is needed.
>
> My children have done their part in providing the state with WASL data. They will be tested no more.

No one ever tried to coerce me to allow my children to take the test. No one tried to tell me the test was worthwhile or that my children would suffer because they lacked test scores. No one harassed or threatened my children when they were not taking the test.

In 2006, all that was missing from my graduates' attire was the "WASL cord" awarded to approximately half their classmates for having passed all sections of the tenth-grade test. But my children were lucky; had they been born two years later and found themselves in the class of 2008, they would have been required to pass the WASL in order to walk with their class and receive a high school diploma.

As of 2009, WASL was no longer the test for Washington State. The acronym has changed, but the high-stakes graduation requirement remains. In younger grades, students who fail the test are placed in remedial classes, removed from electives, and denied entry to special programs.

Parents are the final line of defense against harmful educational policy. Parents have the right and the responsibility to protect their children from irresponsible, invalid, unproven practice. Resistance on the part of parents is never futile. In fact, just saying no is the only sure thing. What if they gave a test and nobody came?

Taking the Battle (and the Buttons) to the "Other" Washington

My own activism has slowed a bit since my children are grown and I've begun working in the field of communication as a college instructor. However, in July 2011, I couldn't resist joining my colleagues from around the nation to march against harmful education policy in Washington, DC, with Save Our Schools. For the occasion, I dusted off the old machine and turned my front room into a button factory once again: "Education is a journey—not a race to the top!" "With Academic Freedom and Justice for All!"

Juanita Doyon is the proud mother of four public school graduates and holds a master's degree in communication and leadership studies from Gonzaga University.

20. "Just Parents" Challenge Mayor Daley, Arne Duncan, and Renaissance 2010

Julie Woestehoff

Two years before he was sworn in as U.S. secretary of education, Arne Duncan sat across from a public school parent in National Public Radio's local Chicago studio. The show was *Talk of the Nation* and the topic was school reform.

Duncan was chief executive officer of the Chicago Public Schools, the third-largest school district in the nation. I was the parent, the executive director of Parents United for Responsible Education. PURE is a tiny nonprofit advocacy group based in Chicago that strongly opposes many of Duncan's policies, ones he initiated in Chicago and now promotes nationwide.

Duncan opened his comments by praising the changes in Chicago's schools since Mayor Richard M. Daley gained control of them in 1995. The radio host took a call from a Florida parent who was concerned that parents' role in the schools would diminish under mayoral control; Duncan answered that Chicago has elected, parent-majority, local school councils through which parents participate in school decision making.

His comment gave me the perfect opening. I agreed with Duncan about local school councils, and mentioned research showing the academic gains in the schools they oversee. Then I added that, unfortunately, under Mayor Daley's Renaissance 2010 plan, the councils were being dismantled and replaced with advisory boards appointed by Duncan and Daley's hand-picked school board. I warned parents to be very concerned about what might happen to their role if the mayor controlled the schools. Duncan was not pleased.

How did "just a public school parent" end up with the opportunity to debate the future education secretary on national radio?

Chicago Parents Win a Seat at the Table

In the fall of 1987, a group of parents and teachers formed a united front during a nineteen-day school strike. Concerned that public officials were not taking proper responsibility for providing all children with a quality education, the group named itself Parents United for Responsible Education, only later noticing the "PURE" acronym. The group held weekly public meetings during the strike. A culminating one-thousand-person march on City Hall convinced Mayor Harold Washington to reopen the schools the next school day. Along with many others, PURE successfully fought for the Chicago School Reform Act of 1988, which established local school councils and processes for collaborative school improvement planning, budgeting, and, where needed, school remediation and intervention.

During the early years of reform, the district administration worked cooperatively with councils and education advocates, and schools began to improve. But some civic leaders were impatient with the rate of improvement, so in 1995 the state legislature recentralized some school authority by allowing Chicago's mayor to appoint the board of education members and a chief executive officer. The head of Chicago's schools would no longer be required to have education credentials.

Fighting the Daley–Duncan Renaissance 2010 Plan

Mayoral control ushered in corporate-style "reform." For the CEO position, Mayor Daley selected his budget director, who promoted policies and practices that have since spread across the country, including high-stakes testing, top-down interventions in "failed" schools, and a so-called business model for education, which opened the door to privatization. PURE challenged these policies from the beginning.

Disappointed that student test scores had flatlined after a brief uptick, Daley replaced his first CEO with the more affable Arne Duncan in 2001. However, the bad-policy bandwagon rolled on.

In 2003, Daley challenged Chicago's philanthropic community to get behind an aggressive new reform plan called Renaissance 2010.

Under this plan, sixty schools would be closed for low performance as determined by test scores, or for low enrollment or dilapidated facilities. One hundred new schools, including charter, "turnaround," and other privately managed schools, were to be opened by 2010. Local businesses and foundations pledged at least $50 million toward this effort. In June 2004, Duncan announced the first list of schools to be closed, including ten elementary schools and one high school.

Once again, PURE got together with teachers and other groups, this time to develop strategies to challenge the closings. During one memorable twenty-four-hour period in August 2004, we staged a major protest before, during, and after the Chicago Board of Education's monthly business meeting. We camped out on the sidewalk outside the school district's Loop headquarters. We stayed there all night so that we would be the first ones in line to sign up to testify during the public participation segment of the board meeting. Others joined us in the early hours, and by 7 a.m. there were about forty of our coalition members in the sign-up line. Reporters from every local TV, radio, and print news outlet showed up. Buses from the schools on the closing list arrived, and parents and staff formed a picket line on the sidewalk outside district headquarters. During the board meeting, our message—stop the school closings—completely dominated the public testimony because so many people from our group had signed up early. However, the board members voted unanimously to close every school on the list.

PURE Tips, Facts, and Perspectives

PURE has always believed that knowledge is power. Parents often just don't know their rights or how to demand the kind of education their children need and deserve. One of PURE's main strategies, then, has been to tell the truth in a brief, user-friendly way.

We developed a one-page format for tips or facts that we use in our parent and local school council workshops. PURE tip sheets offer advice about how to do something—prepare for a parent-teacher conference, run a local school council meeting, volunteer at the school, or observe in a classroom. PURE fact sheets explain an issue, list parents' legal rights, summarize an education law, and so on. The fact sheets became increasingly important in our advocacy work as the mayor and Duncan began to make unsubstantiated claims and spread disinformation about their policies, and we saw that no one else in Chicago was challenging them effectively.

Finally, we created "PURE Perspectives," which combines facts with analysis of various issues. This was the beginning of our blog, "PURE Thoughts."

PURE's Perspective: Arne Duncan "Dodges" the Truth

One of the first PURE fact sheets to address Renaissance 2010 was "The Problem with Charter Schools," which exploded six common myths about charter schools. (This, along with other resources, is available on the *Educational Courage* website.) In another, we summarized the 2009 Stanford/Credo report on charter schools, which found that African American and Latino students do worse in Illinois charters, almost all of which are in Chicago.

Despite the expensive public relations campaign promoting charters, we and others were effective to the extent that Duncan backtracked, claiming that he only supported "good" charter schools. Unfortunately, his Race to the Top program and Blueprint for Education Reform still demand nearly unlimited charter expansion.

We've also tracked Chicago's "turnaround" schools, beginning with Dodge Renaissance Academy, which President Obama chose as the site to announce Duncan's nomination for secretary of education. The former Dodge Elementary School had been closed in 2002 and remained closed for a year of restructuring, while a private management company, Academy of Urban School Leaders (AUSL), gave the building a facelift and hired and trained a completely new staff. The school reopened as Dodge Renaissance Academy in 2004. Test scores at the school increased markedly; in 2006, Dodge logged the city's largest overall state test-score increase.

When those scores came out, Duncan proudly announced them and added some even more impressive news—that Dodge

Renaissance Academy had nearly doubled the achievement growth of the students who had been at Dodge before it closed. PURE decided to look a little closer at this seeming miracle. We sent an e-mail to the district communications department asking for the data behind these remarkable claims. It sent us an internal memo that included a key piece of information Duncan had not mentioned—only 20 of the 336 students who were enrolled at Dodge the year it was closed came back to the school when it reopened. The following year, there were only twelve original students left. The claims of great success were based on data from only a dozen students. Not only did this make the district's grandiose claims meaningless, but it raised a disturbing question: what had happened to the former Dodge students?

We called that fact sheet "Dodge-ing the Truth," and noted that Renaissance 2010 turnarounds seemed to be more about changing the student body than improving the quality of education.

The Fight Goes Nationwide

When Duncan took a pre-nomination media tour prior to his appointment as education secretary, we were well prepared to weigh in on the wisdom of taking Daley-Duncan's school reform style nationwide. We summarized some of the main problems with Duncan's signature program in our fact sheet, "Top Ten Reasons Why Renaissance 2010 is a Failure." PURE posted a detailed refutation of a 2009 Duncan speech to the National Press Club in which he touted Dodge and other Chicago "miracles." A few days later, *Education Week* published an essay Duncan had written, which repeated several of these whoppers. Three weeks later, it published PURE's letter challenging his statements.

PURE has been punished for its strong stand against corporate reform and school privatization. Financial support from local foundations has disappeared, and we have seen much of that support go to a handful of "Astroturf" parent groups. Astroturf organizing is an effort to manipulate the public on a specific issue by giving a false appearance of grassroots involvement. In Chicago, Astroturf groups have organized to "educate" parents about the terrible state of their neighborhood schools and the wonderful charter school alternative.

Instead of giving up, however, PURE has held on and even developed a national presence. We are now the Midwest hub of Parents Across America (PAA), a national group that advocates for better public schools for all children. PAA started with a meeting between me and Leonie Haimson, a parent activist from New York City. When the mayor of Los Angeles started to talk about gaining control of LA schools, Leonie and I wrote a joint letter from New York City and Chicago to LA parents advising them to fight the takeover. The mayors of New York and Chicago issued a joint refutation of our letter. Next, we wrote a joint letter critiquing the Obama administration's Blueprint for Education Reform and the lack of parent input into federal education policy. This letter was published in *Education Week*.

Soon, other active parents from across the country began to reach out to us, and we decided to create PAA. We have written our own parent blueprint for education reform, which has been endorsed by many other groups. Our network includes members from numerous states. We find that when a member in one city or district has a problem, members from another area often have a solution.

We believe that the antidote to the attack on our schools is more organizing, more parent voice, more community action, and more truth telling. PURE intends to be around for a long time to make sure that happens.

Julie Woestehoff is the executive director of Parents United for Responsible Education and cofounder of Parents Across America, which work to bring parents' voices into school policymaking.

21. From Seeds to Fruition: The Making of a Resistance Movement

Don Perl

I was faced with the prospect of preparing my eighth-grade students for high-stakes standardized testing in the fall of 2000—the test to be administered in February 2001. The more I studied this concept of high-stakes testing, the more abhorrent it became to me, and the more I saw it as a violation of my egalitarian principles as an educator. I was teaching in an inner-city middle school in Greeley, Colorado, the population of which was about 50 percent Latina/o. After much deliberation and study, I decided that I could not in good conscience administer the Colorado Student Assessment Program (CSAP) testing to my students.

In January 2001, on the day we honor the memory of Dr. Martin Luther King Jr., I sent letters to policymakers, legislators, the local and state school boards, and the governor's office stating the reasons for my boycott. My letter set forth two concepts: the tests are antithetical to the egalitarian premise of public schools, and they undermine the dignity of the teaching profession.

With these letters and with that refusal, the seeds of our Coalition for Better Education were planted, although I did not know it at the time. I was suspended for two weeks without pay during the administration of CSAP tests. When I returned, I found the atmosphere so oppressive that I decided to make that year my last.

In 2002, I began teaching Spanish at a local university in the Department of Hispanic Studies. My new colleagues encouraged me to keep speaking out against the injustices of standardized testing. I developed a brochure consolidating these injustices, in both English and Spanish, and became a town crier at an educational fiesta and at the celebration of the Mexican Independence Day each September.

At that celebration in September 2003, a colleague approached the booth that some fellow teachers and I had organized, read our brochure, and said, "Don, why don't you try to get the elimination of CSAP on the ballot?" That brief conversation inspired me to investigate the possibility of a ballot initiative for that fall's election. Various phone calls and a statement of intent to the Office of the Secretary of State resulted in conferences with the Legislative Council.

What followed was the tedious process of researching school law and drafting legislative language to counter the legislation already on the books that used CSAP results to determine additional funding for schools. Originally, funds were to be established to reward those schools with high scores and to help those schools with low scores. However, that cache was never funded, so the entire regimen turned into a punishment of schools with low scores. I met with the Legislative Council on three occasions in the winter of 2004 to refine the language of our ballot initiative so that it conformed to state requirements of clearly addressing a single issue.

Early in March 2004, the Office of the Secretary of State invited me to meet with a panel of three to discuss the proposed ballot initiative. The initiative, as proposed, was projected on a screen in a conference room. The panel asked me to read it and make any requested changes before they would pass judgment on it. Essentially, it proposed an amendment to the Colorado Revised Statutes that set forth the elimination of CSAP testing as an instrument to classify schools.

The panel conferred for a few moments, and then the person in charge turned to me and said, "Mr. Perl, your ballot initiative, number 83, has been approved. All signatures must be submitted to this office on or before August 2 of this year."

How were we ever going to get the required sixty-seven thousand signatures? The thought rumbled around in my head that professional educators would be the first to sign. How wrong I was! I contacted the leaders of the Colorado Education Association. Their newsletter had always published articles stridently criticizing the one-size-fits-all formula of CSAP testing. "We've done your work for you," I said in a telephone conversation with the vice president. "We now have a ballot initiative seeking the elimination of CSAP.

With your support, we can get this on the ballot. You could encourage all members of the association to sign. And we can turn the wheel of history for the good of our children." There was total silence on the other end. Then, the vice president said, "Don, we can't support this initiative." Now it was my turn to be silent. Finally, I said, "How can you rage against CSAP in your newsletter, and not support this initiative?" "It's politics, Don. Good luck." End of conversation.

Nonetheless, we did get some media coverage, and some parents called to say that they wanted to help. Would I be willing to send them petitions? I developed what I now call "revolutionary headquarters" in my house, and I sent petitions to people with notes that said, "Get as many signatures as you can and send them back well before the 2nd of August." We had what amounted to four months to get signatures. Channel 9 News took a mild interest in our efforts. A reporter and photographer showed up at revolutionary headquarters to do an interview and take pictures. I don't think they were too impressed. A small piece ran the following day on its website.

Still, the word spread. Many folks called to say that they had had no idea about this ballot initiative until they had read the spot on the Channel 9 news website or heard the piece on public radio, so a number of parents participated in getting signatures. All of the signature gatherers were volunteers: parents, a professor, a public defender, and a few students from the University of Northern Colorado. Our goal was to give the Secretary of State something to count.

On August 2, we met at the Office of the Secretary of State. I had sent the word out saying, "Let's make this a media event." Some thirty signature gatherers and the media converged at the office. We all handed in our petitions. The media took pictures, did interviews, and then left. We, the signature gatherers, were left alone with our thoughts. Of course, we knew that we did not have enough signatures to make the ballot, but we did want to build on the momentum we had created. Two weeks later, we received word that we had gathered 12,485 signatures, impressive considering our very limited resources.

Back at the Office of the Secretary of State on that August 2, the question became, "What do we do now?" Some students from the

University of Northern Colorado, where I was teaching and where I had given presentations on the harms of high-stakes standardized testing, had created a website and labeled the mission to inform the public of these harms, the Coalition for Better Education (CBE). Although the site was primitive, at least it provided a point of departure for activism. We, the signature gatherers, the activists, sat in the waiting room of the Secretary of State's Office and brainstormed about the question. We could advertise on our website. Or we could check into media advertising. Thus, the idea of advertising on billboards took form. A parent then stepped forward and volunteered to make political buttons to support and augment the advertising campaign.

I studied certain texts of the Colorado Revised Statutes and pertinent case law. We could definitely make the case that parents have the last say in their children's education and could exempt their children from CSAP. Thus, we developed the message for our advertising, "Parents, We CAN do something about this injustice. Opt-out letters at www.thecbe.org."

We have raised money for this advertising every year, beginning in the spring of 2005. The CBE website now has a photograph of the billboards as they appear each year along Colorado highways. Parents have spoken out and opted their children out of the tests. Administrators, often threatened by parents taking action, have resorted to their own bullying practices to attempt to force compliance.

In the legislative session in the spring of 2008, Representative Judy Solano from Brighton, Colorado, sponsored a bill that would require school districts to inform parents of their exemption rights and require that no negative consequences follow from exercising such an option. This was the second time that Representative Solano sponsored the bill. This time, the bill received much support. Our coalition was on the frontlines in that piece of legislation, and in March 2008, more than forty of our parents, teachers, and public school students appeared and testified before the Senate and House Education Committees in favor of this legislation. Everyone's experiences differed, of course, but their messages were clear and heartfelt. I was impressed with the young people who came forward. They were the ones who spoke most eloquently about the high-stakes testing movement that was so insulting to them, so stressful, so antithetical to educational principles, and thus so devastating to the public schools. The legislation passed both houses and went to the governor's desk for signature.

In June 2008, after both houses had adjourned for the summer, Governor Bill Ritter vetoed the bill, a move that stunned us. In 2009, Representative Solano again attempted to reintroduce the legislation. It died in committee. Our energies were exhausted.

Now the torch is being passed. CBE colleagues such as Angela Engel, Conny Jensen, Sylvia Martínez, and Nina Bishop, to name only four, continue to sound the alarm. Angela has written *Seeds of Tomorrow: Solutions for Improving Our Children's Education,* a book designed to inform and support parents. Conny Jensen, Sylvia Martínez, and Nina Bishop have become strong examples of parents advocating for children. There are many others.

More and more, parents now see their children's lives damaged and limited by the inhumanity of high-stakes standardized testing. Our coalition's letterhead bears the motto, "Created to dignify the autonomy of our children and of their teachers." This message needs to resonate ever more widely in a political climate increasingly insensitive to the needs and talents of children and to the critical role that professional educators play in bringing out the best in their children.

As of this writing, public education faces an even more formidable force; with vast resources, current secretary of education Arne Duncan is imposing strict national standards under the rallying cry of Race to the Top. Our coalition has taken an active role in speaking out against these further efforts to elevate competition above cooperation and to bribe school districts into conforming to a dehumanizing agenda. In the fall of 2010 and again in the spring of 2011, the CBE showed the film, *Race to Nowhere* to audiences of parents, teachers, aspiring teachers, and their professors.

I have had the life-altering experience of practicing two professions, law and education. The first profession, in my experience, emphasizes competition and is long on bluster. As a practitioner,

I struggled with the concept that competition is intrinsically good, something to be exalted at almost any price. I see my second profession, education, as far more noble in that ideally it recognizes the individuality of the learner and seeks to use the talents and interests of the student to connect with the curriculum. In short, the profession is one of love.

However, something heartless in our society labels love as nothing to be trumpeted. Teachers, generally, are humble about their noble qualities, while attorneys, I have experienced, have no inhibitions about boasting of their own shallow ones. It is teachers' humility that is responsible, sadly, for the quagmire of public education. Mahatma Gandhi and Dr. Martin Luther King Jr. understood the power of love. Richard Lakin, educator and author of *Teaching as an Act of Love,* writes, "Teaching is first and foremost an act of love." Noted scholar and activist Susan Ohanian, author of *One Size Fits Few* and *Why Is Corporate America Bashing Our Public Schools?,* also emphasizes the importance of love in our profession: "Loving forlorn children gives them life and possibility. Teaching is love in action, requiring no credentials." Once the profession recognizes the critical role that love plays in our relationships with children, once classroom professionals realize that we must speak for the students because we know how, then we can begin the arduous, but wonderful journey toward the renaissance of a profession.

I have learned in the course of these last ten years that what individuals do locally is critical. The lessons in analytical thought, courage, and commitment that we instill in our children and the lessons in mindfully speaking on their behalf can be inspiring beyond our imagining. Let us remember that we send our children to school to become more human, to learn to cooperate in a society that needs cooperation for survival. Let us remember that our mission is to instill compassion in a world hungering for it. And let us remember that we send our children to learn nurturing skills essential for the survival of all of us on this fragile planet. And let us spread the word.

In July 2011, the Coalition for Better Education organized a northern Colorado version of the national Save Our Schools march and rally. The words of the late Reverend Steve Brown resonated throughout the gathering, "Whoever knows what snowflake causes the avalanche, or what word prevents further injustice?" Let these words be an inspiration for all of us who raise our voices for children.

_____

Don Perl is a lifetime educator who has taught both in the United States and abroad. He presently teaches Spanish at the University of Northern Colorado.

22. Making a Difference

Jane Hirschmann, Ujju Aggarwal, and Donna Nevel

Parent organizing can and does take many different shapes and forms. As with all organizing, it is strongest when it begins from the ground up, with people's own stories and lived experiences. Ensuring that the leadership of those most affected by injustice remains at the center of all levels of organizing is critical—from documenting what is wrong with public education to determining strategy to effectively move forward and create change. This has now become even more important when families, particularly low-income parents and students of color, and educators are increasingly shut out of decision making that affects our schools and public education system. We need schools that reflect, respect, and serve their communities and a *public* education system that encourages all students and communities to flourish.

We present here two different examples of parents organizing for justice in public education in New York City. The first, written by Jane Hirschmann, is about challenging high-stakes testing, and the second, by Ujju Aggarwal and Donna Nevel, is about fighting for equity in an increasingly segregated and unequal school district. Both stories provide examples of parents organizing to resist destructive educational policies and practices that increasingly use the rhetoric of choice, accountability, and "reform."

Time Out From Testing

Jane Hirschmann

Parents in twenty-eight New York high schools that belong to the New York Performance Standards Consortium (the Consortium) formed a group called Time Out From Testing (TOFT) to protect the performance-based assessment system used in our children's schools, sometimes known as "portfolio assessment." The system is used in lieu of one-size-fits-all high-stakes tests.

We began by holding meetings in our schools where we spoke with other parents about the impact that high-stakes Regents exams would have if we lost the opportunity to assess students by demonstrating what children know and can do. Parents together with teachers and principals designed actions and strategies to gain support for a system that did not rely on high-stakes standardized tests.

Our campaign included writing informational flyers in multiple languages and letter writing, educating government officials, cultivating the press and interested lawmakers, holding press briefings, filing a lawsuit against the New York State Education Department, and reaching out to and gaining support from one of the most powerful unions in the city—1199 Health and Hospital Workers Union (SEIU)—whose members' children attended some of the Consortium schools. We helped write legislation in favor of performance-based assessment.

In order to get this legislation passed, we organized a major rally in the State Capitol to demonstrate to lawmakers that parents, teachers, and students were determined to protect a system of assessment that did not undermine challenging curriculum and engaging instruction. Two thousand of us, representing thousands more, went to Albany and made the argument that high-stakes tests dumb down the curriculum, force teachers to teach to the test, and shortchange our children's education.

A three-hour bus ride to the Albany rally provided us an opportunity to build team spirit, role play, and develop talking points to use in meetings with state officials. We grouped parents with teachers and students to visit key members of the Assembly and Senate. We even handed out fortune cookies to legislators with our messages inside. Following each of these meetings, we debriefed and made lists of those legislators who supported us and those who needed additional visits. The legislation obtained overwhelmingly bipartisan support from the N.Y. State Senate but never got to the floor of the Assembly.

However, in the end, we won. The Senate, the Assembly, the Board of Regents, and the Consortium reached a compromise. They agreed that the Consortium's system of performance-based assessment would remain in place. Consortium schools are required to give only the English Language Arts Regents. All other subject areas continue to be assessed based on performance.

The next campaign resulted from Mayor Michael Bloomberg's attempt to tie third graders' promotions directly to their standardized test scores. The mayor's rationale was to end so-called "social promotion," a policy of promoting students even if they have not mastered the material in order to keep them with students of their own age. Despite the efforts by parents and educators to dissuade school officials from using test scores so narrowly, the mayor and the chancellor introduced a rigid promotion policy that ignored the fact that the city did not actually have a social promotion policy. The truth was that 40 percent of New York City's high school students entered ninth grade over age. Why? Because they had been held back sometime before they had reached ninth grade. The press never questioned or investigated whether social promotion actually existed. When journalists finally had a closer look at the resulting data, they found that what Time Out From Testing had been saying was correct: a high percentage of children had repeated grades. Misinformation and misrepresentation had resulted in poor policy decisions.

For this campaign, we decided that parents should write letters to the mayor and school principals expressing their opposition to third-grade high-stakes testing. TOFT reached out to national educational experts to gain support for opposing high-stakes tests in early childhood grades and prepared press releases to inform the media.

The mayor and the Department of Education ultimately implemented high-stakes testing for third graders. However, parents' organizing efforts established an appeals process that includes the use of a child's portfolio of work in cases where there is a dispute. This, at least, allows for greater flexibility than the mayor's original policy.

Since the press played such an important role in shaping public opinion, it was vital to cultivate individual reporters assigned to our specific beat, educate them, and keep in touch with them over the long haul. As reporters are reassigned, we must repeat this process with each new reporter.

Time Out From Testing grew from the need for parents to protect children's education. Sometimes it is the fight to stop high-stakes testing in the lower grades or the unfair practice of basing 85 percent of a school's report card grade on children's test scores. Sometimes it is the task of educating the public about the injustices of high-stakes testing scores being linked to principals' or teachers' bonuses, teachers' tenure decisions, or admissions to particular schools. The underlying principle always is that parents determine the issues and then TOFT gets involved.

We have learned many important lessons over the years. First and foremost, parents' voices are essential. We must be at the forefront. Second, educators must be involved with us. We share a goal: to support quality education for all children. Therefore, we need to collaborate with one another. Third, it is crucial to work the system by figuring out who the power brokers are, gaining their support, cultivating the press, finding allies in the community, and working to broaden our base. And finally, we have come to understand that change takes time, persistence is critical, and shortcuts usually don't work. Also, it's important to be creative and have fun.

We learned to beware of the language used to promote various agendas. In this, the age of so-called "school reform," the language of change and progress has been co-opted. "Equity," "high standards," "closing the achievement gap," "accountability"—these terms have come to mean different things to different people. So, we need to ensure we understand the implications of any proposed policies for change—and who those changes serve.

Time Out From Testing's hope is that high-stakes tests will be replaced by authentic assessments in which children can demonstrate what they know. This would lead to real school reform.

Challenging Segregation and Inequality in OUR Public Schools

Ujju Aggarwal and Donna Nevel

The Center for Immigrant Families' (CIF) Project to Challenge Segregation in OUR Public Schools is a collectively run organization of low-income immigrant women of color and community members in Manhattan Valley (New York City) that organizes to transform the conditions of injustice facing our communities. This project addresses how our schools have become contested institutions within the context of a community undergoing gentrification and the myriad ways that the public schools have been marketed. This includes privatization mechanisms such as charter schools and voucher programs as well as the creation of segregated enclaves that allow for the establishment of pseudo-private schools within the public school system. At the center of this organizing project was a united community determined to reclaim its public schools. We want to share two lessons from our work that highlight the importance of: (1) an organizing frame and storytelling, not as a discrete or onetime act, but as woven throughout an organizing project; and (2) clarity of intention when engaging the "powers that be."

Frames and Stories

CIF is rooted in popular education, which begins with peoples' own wisdom, knowledge, and experiences. Popular education is a participatory and group-driven process that asks (instead of tells) why. It provides a way for patterns among individual stories to be identified and lead to new analyses, perspectives, and strategies for collective action.

CIF's Project to Challenge Segregation in OUR Public Schools emerged from the Women's Popular Education Program, in which we identified how the dreams that members held for their children's education differed from the realities they faced in the public schools. As we delved deeper into these stories, a common theme of segregation and inequality emerged. We realized that our stories were not new. We began by learning about the history of segregated education and the movements that have worked for desegregation. Rooting ourselves in this legacy informed the vision that would drive our organizing forward.

We also started talking to other community members. Our goal was to understand how de facto segregation was occurring in our district. We soon recognized that there was something else going on. Injustice in education didn't stand out from injustice in other parts of people's daily lives, and segregation had become normalized. Challenging this sentiment that segregated and unequal schools were "just the way things are" became a central focus of our work. We had been doing interviews and surveys, but thought more was needed. Allies trained us in Theatre of the Oppressed techniques, and we developed skits drawing upon one of its forms, street theater. Our skits portrayed members' experiences of being turned away from schools (in both subtle and unsubtle ways) and contrasted this with the treatment of middle- or upper-income and white parents, who were often courted and encouraged to apply.

As we began sharing our street theater, something started to shift. The stories poured out, as hundreds of parents identified with the experiences being portrayed. Parents reported being told to go to schools further uptown where there were more families "like them," being denied translation services, and being asked "how much they could contribute," meaning financial contributions. By documenting these stories, we were able to identify common threads of experience concerning the ways that low-income parents of color were being shut out of our schools. We identified these shared experiences as "mechanisms of exclusion" in our self-published report, *Segregated and Unequal: The Public Elementary Schools of District 3 in NYC.*

We also challenged the pervasive notion that parents or caretakers should be concerned only with their own child and drew upon traditions within working-class communities of color of collective participation in caring for one another's children. Through this frame of collective care and collective responsibility, we were able to build a powerful community response that demanded that all children be valued and encouraged to flourish.

Engaging the Powers That Be

We have identified three examples of "engaging the powers that be" that resulted from years of organizing work.

The first example is from a meeting called by the district's superintendent for elementary school principals to discuss our report's findings. Though the superintendent expected one or two representatives from CIF, we decided to go as a group that included staff organizers, collective members, and parent leaders. We also performed our street theater as part of our presentation. These decisions ensured that what we presented and how we presented it reflected our practice of shared leadership and of centering members' experiences. We also believe we more effectively communicated the issues than if we had just sent one or two representatives to discuss our findings.

The second example is that, as a result of our organizing, New York City Chancellor Joel Klein was forced to admit that the current system was "inequitable and needed to be changed" and called for a district task force on admission procedures. The chancellor asked CIF to be on the task force. Instead of allowing ourselves to be tokenized, we used the opportunity to create an opening for increased representation, and explained that our participation was contingent on the inclusion of other community organizations and Head Start centers in the district in the task force.

In the final example, a uniform admissions policy was created by the Department of Education. As a result, parents could no longer gain access to schools through social networks or economic wealth. While we received a lot of attention for this victory and believe that this was an important beginning, we also think there was another equally important gain. Members spoke of finally being treated with respect, of feeling that power was shifting in the community. Parents were going to schools in teams, addressing unequal treatment and refusing to be ignored, and schools started to recognize that this community was claiming rights and building power. As we know too well, policies can be overturned with the stroke of a pen, mutated, and "reformed." However, when a community has engaged in a process of transformation in which it reclaims its own sense of power and its strength, the effects cannot be undone. And it is this power that continues to grow and expand as we organize to take back and transform our public schools.

Jane Hirschmann, a public-education organizer and social justice activist on local, national, and international issues, is the cofounder and chair of Time Out From Testing.

Ujju Aggarwal is a community organizer and a doctoral student at City University of New York Graduate Center. Donna Nevel, a community psychologist and educator, coordinates the Participatory Action Research Center for Education Organizing.

23. What Endures: Meaningful Assessment for the Long Haul

Chris W. Gallagher and Doug Christensen

Overture

Myles Horton was an angry man. Coming of age in Tennessee during the Great Depression, he was on intimate terms with racial and economic injustice. According to his autobiography, *The Long Haul*, he faced many setbacks as he struggled to establish and keep open his Highlander Folk School, which taught leadership skills to workers of all races. Throughout his long career as an educator and activist, his school, his livelihood, and even his life were threatened repeatedly by bigots and defenders of the powerful, including state officials bent on closing his "radical" school. He lost friends and students he trained for the civil rights movement, including Martin Luther King Jr.

But Horton knew what he had to do:

> I had to turn my anger into a slow burning fire, instead of a consuming fire. You don't want the fire to go out—you never let it go out—and if it ever gets weak, you stoke it, but you don't want it to burn you up. It keeps you going, but you subdue it, because you don't want to be destroyed by it.[1]

Horton knew democracy is a long-term project. So he devoted his life to the patient pursuit of democratic education, trusting that "[w]hat people need are experiences in democracy, in making democratic decisions that affect their lives and communities."[2]

As a former state commissioner of education and a professor, our lives are very different from Horton's. But like him, we have devoted ourselves to democratic education. We too have faced our share of setbacks, including the dismantling of a statewide assessment system we valued in favor of state tests. And we too have struggled to keep our fires smoldering, rather than allowing them to consume us. This essay is an attempt to do just that. We examine what endures when the consuming fire is extinguished and we can see by the clearer light of the smoldering fire.

Specifically, we describe our idea of meaningful assessment for the long haul. We want to train your eyes on the future, helping you move toward (or stick with) meaningful assessment no matter what the political winds bring. Those winds might stoke your fires or threaten to extinguish them. But meaningful assessment is always possible if we focus on what endures: vision, hope, resolve.

Vision

We remember:

> A high school student—all confidence and poise—ushers school visitors to the various Science Day displays, explaining the principles and procedures involved in each project or asking the student-scientists to do so. Each display, he points out, includes a self-assessment written by the scientist. The group stops at a beat-frequency project, and the guide asks his "colleague" to explain the principle. She does, with the help of a sound clip of jet engines. Impressed, a visitor admits she remembers "almost nothing" from her high school science classes. "I think we'll remember," the student-guide replies. The scientist agrees.

> A team of teachers gathers around a conference table. English teacher: "Which essay did you think was strongest?" History teacher: "Mark's." (Others nod.) English teacher: "I liked Mark's, too. Now let's see if we can identify what's really working in the essay." Social studies teacher: "Mark's essay stands out to me because it really tries to say something." English teacher: "Agreed. Now let's think about what to call this and how to teach it."

Parents, aunts and uncles, and tribal elders gather this evening in the gymnasium to hear students present their graduation portfolios. They listen quietly, respectfully. After each presentation, a question, maybe two, from community members: "What did you like learning most? What was the hardest thing about school? What will you do when you graduate? Can I see your portfolio?"

A state assessment director visits a small school. The school assessment team leader immediately pulls out reams of paper, begins running down data. "Wait," says the assessment director. "First, let's talk. Tell me what you're doing in your school. Tell me what's going well and what I can help you with. Let me talk to some other teachers, too. Then we can talk numbers."

What endures for us is a vision of meaningful assessment: student-involved, teacher-led, community-based, and policy-supported.

Where to start? Where you (all of you) are.

If you ever lose track of where people are in the process, then you have no relationship to them and there's nothing you can do. So if you have to make a choice between moving in the direction you want to move people, and working with them where they are, you always choose to work with them where they are.[3]

Just as important as *where* to start is *who* starts. To this, we say: everyone. Begin, as always, with students and move outward: How can they become observers of and informants about their own learning? How can teachers design classroom assessments that must form the backbone of any meaningful assessment system? How can administrators and policymakers act as support staff for teachers, providing conditions in which assessment nourishes teaching and learning? How can parents and community members bring their perspectives to assessment activities? And how can you all pull in the same direction, from where you are to where you'd like to be? A vision for meaningful assessment is multiple yet shared. *E pluribus unum.*

Hope

We remember:

> A panel of students addresses a ballroom full of educators. "The thing about self-assessment," the high schooler says, "is that it forces you to know what you know." The other panelists giggle. Then the sixth grader pipes up: "That sounds funny. But it's true. My teacher says, 'You have to know that you know, and I need to know that you know that you know.'"

> A first-year teacher shares a classroom assessment with her professional learning community. A colleague wants to know how she learned how to design such good assessments. "I had lots of practice in my education courses," the teacher says. "We were taught that assessment is part of teaching and learning, so we did assessment in almost every course."

> A school administrator scraps a professional development session to give teachers more time to work on their assessments. "They just need to talk," he tells a visitor. "Good things happen when teachers teach each other."

What endures for us is hope for meaningful assessment: reflection, integration, collaboration, and confidence.

How does vision become reality? Trust is crucial:

> It's the kind of thing you just have to posit: you have to have trust in people, and you have to work through it to the place

where people respond to that trust. Then you have to believe that people have the capacity within themselves to develop the ability to govern themselves.[4]

Trust that students can be taught to be reliable observers of and informants about their own learning. Trust that teachers can learn to develop valid and reliable assessments. Trust that administrators and policymakers can learn to facilitate vibrant school cultures of inquiry and innovation. This will take work, but it is impossible if you don't first trust that it is possible. Meaningful assessment is fed by hope.

Resolve
We remember:

A teacher looks state senators in the eye: "Classroom-based assessment is the best thing to happen in my thirty years of education. Please do not take this away from us—from our kids."

A parent addresses her local school board: "Prove to me these tests help my child learn. I won't have them put through another battery of tests just so the school can look good."

A school administrator faces down his local chamber of commerce: "Here's my pledge: I will never make my teachers administer an assessment they did not have a hand in creating."

A state commissioner of education squares off against federal policymakers: "Assessment belongs in teachers' hands; there will be no state tests while I'm commissioner."

What endures for us is resolve for meaningful assessment: courage, persistence, purpose, and conviction.

How to stay on the path for the long haul? Remember first principles:

We've changed methods and techniques over the years, but the philosophy and conditions for learning stay the same. There is no method to learn from Highlander [Folk School]. What we do involves trusting people and believing in their ability to think for themselves.[5]

Our first principle is an integral part of teaching and learning, embedded in both. It is an instructional tool, not a policy weapon. Students and teachers are the most important users of assessment. Teachers *can* design and implement assessments of high technical quality. The purpose of assessment is to inform good judgment and sound decision making, starting in the classroom. Everyone has a role in shaping environments conducive to meaningful assessment.

There is strength in these principles, and there is strength to be drawn from them. Use your first principles to keep yourself honest; test your decisions against them. Use your fire to temper them, to toughen them, and they will return the favor: in them, you will find the resiliency required for the long haul.

Coda

Horton knew to learn from the birds:

Birds will take advantage of a tailwind, and when the wind is blowing the other way, they'll hole up. They won't exhaust their strength going against that wind for long when they'd make only a few miles a day or get blown backward. They rest, because if they rest that day and restore their strength, the next day they can much more than make up for what they lost by not going. . . . They change their course year after year on the basis of the particular situation. They never come back exactly the same way twice because the conditions are never the same, but they always get to their destination. They have a purpose, a goal. They know where they are going, but they zigzag and they change tactics according to the situation.[6]

Go when the going's good; wait when it's not. Rely on your vision, hope, and resolve. You will need them—*we will need them*—for the long haul.

Chris W. Gallagher is professor of English and Writing Program director at Northeastern University. Doug Christensen is emeritus commissioner of education in Nebraska, having served fourteen years in that role, and is now professor of leadership in education in the Graduate Division of Doane College.

Notes

1. Quotes in this essay are from Myles Horton, *The Long Haul: An Autobiography* (New York: Teachers College Press, 1999), 80.
2. Ibid., 133.
3. Ibid., 132.
4. Ibid., 8.
5. Ibid., 157.
6. Ibid., 198–99.

24. Voices of Activism

Many educators, students, and parents have joined together in coalitions that link the fight to preserve public education with other efforts that challenge inequality in our society. Encouragingly, recent actions to fight for more democratic schools in a democratic society have become larger, broader, and more public.

We share here the voices of some of the thousands of people involved in such coalitions and actions. They demonstrate that expanded strategies for change—public demonstrations, social justice unionism, and civil disobedience—have the potential for building renewed educational activism that is part of collective movement to regain democratic schools and a democratic society.

Arizona Students Protest New Law
Banning Ethnic Studies Classes

In the spring of 2010, Arizona governor Jan Brewer signed a new law banning ethnic studies in Arizona public schools (HB 2281). The law would shut down the popular Mexican American/Raza Studies Program in the Tucson school district. It would also affect specialized courses in African American and Native American studies. In response, students took to the streets to voice their opposition to the bill. Fifteen people, most of them students, were arrested protesting the law at the state offices of education in Tucson soon after it was signed.

Kim Dominguez was one of those arrested. She's a graduate of Raza Studies. In an edited excerpt of an interview with Kim on *Democracy Now!*, the day after her arrest, she describes why she was willing to publicly take a stand and face arrest:

> I think the whole community and fellow students were supportive of the arrests. . . . The intentions were to do the right thing and to ignite a spark within the nation. . . . We have to move to the next step to protect these classes, to protect our

communities against HB 2281, SB 1070. We've done petitions. We've done letters. We've done calls. We've done everything that this American United States system has asked us to do. We vote. I vote. I think it's time to move to the next step.

I think the community was supportive of us moving it to the next step. It's not just about ethnic studies. It's not just about SB 1070. It's beyond that. This is a blatant attack on the Latino, Mexicano, Chicana indigenous community and we're stepping up our game. The students are not going to take this kind of violation of our community's rights. . . .

Being arrested really means nothing to me. It's doing the right thing. . . . Having a record . . . it's really a minor thing [compared to] the attacks that I feel every day and the attacks that our communities feel. People are crossing the desert and dying. There are kids all over this country who don't identify with their curly hair, their dark skin, their literature, their parents, their Chicano culture, their indigenous culture, and I think those things are far worse than being arrested. It's just something that happened because we took a stand. . . . I offered a small piece of myself to the community.

Wisconsin Uprising

Bob Peterson, Stephanie Walters, and Kathy M. Xiong

Wisconsin governor Scott Walker declared war on teachers and other public-sector workers on Friday, February 11, 2011. Most of us activists knew when the Republicans swept both chambers of the state legislature and the governorship that things would get bad, but few dreamed they'd get this bad, this fast.

Walker claimed his "budget repair" bill was needed to fill a $137 million shortfall in the state budget, and blamed the crisis on excessive pension and health insurance benefits for public employees. His solution: a frontal attack on the right to organize. His 144-page bill bans all unions in the state university system, at the University of

Wisconsin–Madison hospital, and among state child-care workers. It essentially eliminates collective bargaining rights for all other public-sector unions, requires that unions have recertification votes annually, and prohibits collecting union dues through payroll deduction. Within thirty minutes of Walker's announcement, the right-wing Club for Growth aired TV commercials in Wisconsin's major media markets. The message: public employees are the "haves" and others in the state are the "have-nots."

Hours after Walker proposed his antiworker plan, he placed the Wisconsin National Guard on alert. He also asked the Republican-controlled Senate and Assembly to pass his proposal immediately. The legislative leaders, who a week before had approved $117 million worth of business tax breaks, put Walker's proposals on the fast track.

But a funny thing happened on the way to passing the bill.

First, there was just a small picket line.

Then, demonstrations on Tuesday, February 15, at the Capitol and the governor's home inspired the four-thousand-member Madison teacher union to shut down schools and turn out to protest the next day. That evening, Mary Bell, president of the Wisconsin Education Association Council, put out a call for "our members and all citizens of Wisconsin to come to Madison both Thursday and Friday to go to the Capitol for peaceful demonstrations."

So many Wisconsin teachers called in sick on Thursday that we shut down twenty-four school districts.

In a stunning gesture, the fourteen Democratic state senators fled Wisconsin, depriving the Senate of a quorum and bringing deliberations to a halt.

By Friday, teachers had forced the school districts to shut down in Milwaukee, Racine, Wausau, and Janesville. And twenty thousand people poured into Madison.

On Saturday, February 19, an estimated thirty-five thousand people gathered at the Capitol and protests spread to dozens of communities across the state. Although most teachers went back to work the following week, tens of thousands of other workers and their families came out to protest.

Capping a second solid week of demonstrations, an estimated one hundred thousand protesters gathered in Madison—the biggest demonstration in the state's history.

The attacks on Wisconsin teachers and other public employees are part of a national agenda to privatize public institutions and destroy public-sector unions, the most robust part of a declining labor movement. Governors in Ohio, Pennsylvania, Indiana, and other states are watching Wisconsin closely.

But the governor has awakened a sleeping giant: we've been joined by ironworkers, firefighters, nurses, postal workers, retired public employees, private-sector unions, hundreds of local elected officials, religious organizations, the NAACP, Voces de la Frontera, and other parent and civic groups.

We wanted to give you a sense of what it has felt like to be part of this extraordinary movement!

—Bob Peterson

The past two weeks have been filled with great excitement! I have been called "sister" by folks with whom I share little in common, except one big thing—union membership. I saw the number of protesters swell every single day for a week. I have been moved to tears by students who marched out of school to protest side by side with their teachers. I have chanted and cheered until I was hoarse. I led a hundred thousand people in what has become our rallying cry: "This is what democracy looks like!"

These past fourteen days have also been dark at times. What will happen to our public schools and public services? When did working for government become a crime? When did working for a union make me a thug? What will happen to our schools, our neighborhoods, our state, should we not prevail in our fight to preserve collective bargaining?

But I generally don't have the luxury of hand-wringing and worry because there is so much organizing to do. We must continue the fight to preserve workers' rights because, quite simply, our neighborhoods, our schools, and our democracy depend on it.

—*Stephanie Walters*

As a first-grade Milwaukee teacher, I have had little sleep since Governor Scott Walker announced his budget-repair bill two weeks ago. That first Monday, I went to work as usual and talked with teacher friends about possibly going to Madison later in the week. The one-sided media reporting and increasing anger among teachers helped me make up my mind. I returned to work on Tuesday and told my teaching partner that I'd be taking a personal day on Wednesday to fight for our rights in Madison. She said: "You go and fight, and you do it for as long as necessary."

At Capitol Square in Madison on Wednesday, we were greeted by an impassioned crowd chanting in support of collective bargaining rights, public schools, health care for poor families, and services for the elderly. The crowd inside the Capitol was as passionate and loud as those outside.

Back in Milwaukee, the superintendent posted an aggressive message to teachers: "Act in good conscience, consider our needy children—many of whom are living in poverty—and report to our classrooms throughout the week as the debate continues in Madison." The media tried to color teachers as selfish, careless, and unprofessional. I knew I was acting in the best interests of public education, but I feared that we might lose our parents as allies. Early Friday morning, one of my parents texted me: "There's no school today. Good for you and good luck in Madison." What a relief! I went off to Madison to fight for her son.

—*Kathy M. Xiong*

The Struggle for Social Justice Unionism in Los Angeles

Sarah Knopp and Gillian Russom

Los Angeles Public Schools have been hit hard by the accountability-driven market "reforms" of the No Child Left Behind policy of the Bush administration and President Obama's Race to the Top. The charter school push here followed in the wake of the testing craze and scripted curricula, and now Los Angeles has the highest number of charters of any district in the nation (though not the highest percentage). In California, these policies have undercut public education; destroyed most remnants of local, democratic control of the schools; and begun a major attack on teacher unions. Teachers in Los Angeles have been confronted with the question of whether our union can remain relevant—and even continue to exist—in the face of these attacks. Some teachers have realized that in order to save the union—and therefore our right to collectively bargain and strike when necessary—we have to transform it. We need a "social justice union," and fighting top-down "reforms" has forced us to begin the process of creating one.

In 1994, *Rethinking Schools* ran an article on social justice unionism. It argued that defending public education will require a new kind of teacher unionism. Social justice teacher unions would (1) vigorously defend the rights of members and involve rank-and-file members in the running of the union; (2) put teachers at the center of agendas for school reform; (3) build strategic alliances with parents and communities; (4) promote antiracist social justice curricula; (5) advocate for a radical restructuring of American education; and (6) educate and mobilize the membership to fight for social justice in all areas of society.

We need this now more than ever before because elements of the education agenda under Race to the Top are designed to take away teachers' collective voices. First, tying teacher evaluations to students' test scores will break down the cooperative nature of education and force teachers to teach to the test. Second, the vast majority of charter schools is nonunion and has a high rate of teacher turnover. If teacher unions continue to operate on the "business unionism" model that has predominated for the past thirty years, they will be rendered irrelevant. Unless unions are part of a new civil rights movement, with parents and students demanding equal access to quality education in this country, public education will likely be gutted, and teacher unions could be broken.

Rosa Jimenez, who received a pink slip at the end of her second year of teaching at Los Angeles High School, explains,

> We need to start looking at the bigger picture. We may be amazing teachers, we may touch a group of students every year—but if you don't realize that there are forces actively trying to destroy public education, then it won't matter. If they go the route of judging teachers by tests, then what you do in the classroom won't matter. You have to look at it from outside your classroom. You may be a great teacher, but you're not an island. The schools we work in are not separate from the communities. What does it matter if these students have a great teacher if their families can't even pay rent?

Similarly, Julie Van Winkle, a first-year English teacher at Leichty Middle School, stepped up to organize protests at her school in 2009:

> Social justice unionism is putting an emphasis on *real* school reform, with specific attention given to issues of race and gender. We have to break the habit of fighting *against* issues—charter schools and standardized tests—and instead fight *for* things. We know that our educational system is not meeting the needs of our students, and we know that charter schools and standardized tests are not the answers to the problem of our public schools. We need to focus on what *is*:

reducing class size, collaboration among teachers *and* with parents, creating a curriculum that fosters critical thinking rather than test-taking strategies, and much more.

Rosa, Julie, and many other rank-and-file teachers are organizing to try to reform our union, United Teachers Los Angeles (UTLA). Many have participated in groups like Progressive Educators for Action, Association of Raza Educators, and other union caucuses and independent social justice groups that are working to transform UTLA. These rank-and-file organizations have created a climate that has encouraged the UTLA leadership to call for some tactics that have moved our union in the right direction. UTLA has a long way to go to become a social justice union. We have not yet figured out how to take the kind of militant—and probably illegal—actions that will be needed to defend our members in this climate. We have not yet built the kind of long-term alliances with communities that will be necessary to force progressive taxation to fund our schools. We have not made social justice curriculum the norm rather than the exception in our schools. However, the implementation of the market-driven reforms is forcing us to move in that direction.

Dipti Baranwal was a new teacher at Manual Arts High School when the attacks began:

> The union is very important for fighting isolation. Participation in the union is a way of challenging the situation in our workplaces—fighting the idea that we have to stay in our classrooms, isolated, with fifty kids at a time. It gives us a sense of collectivity, and also a way to acknowledge the nature of our work—that it's very human, and that we're working with young people. I think that unions are necessary, that they're usable, but that they're not the only structures that we need. I'm very strongly invested in the union but I also do work outside it.

Real educational reform will come when the demands raised by social movements combine with unions that have the power to make the system heed those demands. While the alliances that we build may begin as a method of defending ourselves from attack, they will no doubt create the forum to discuss what real justice will mean and how we can get it.

A Nationwide Movement to Save Our Schools

Brian Jones

On Saturday, July 30, 2011, I participated in the Save Our Schools (SOS) march in Washington, DC, alongside thousands of educators, parents, students, and activists. We came from all parts of the country, united by outrage with federal education policy and local school budget cuts.

The messages on countless homemade signs spoke clearly to the growing frustration with privatization, attacks on teacher unions, and, especially, the use of high-stakes standardized tests to measure student achievement and, increasingly, teacher effectiveness. "Spend $ on kids, not te$t$!" read one sign; another, "Education > testing." My personal favorite wasn't a placard or banner, but a mock graveyard arranged near the rally site where tombstones indicated that Joy, Creativity, Cooperation, and Critical Thinking were among the deceased.

I had traveled to DC from New York City with a group of educators and parents from the Grassroots Education Movement. At the pre-march SOS conference, our workshop (on building a grassroots movement to defend public education) was well attended, and our film, *The Inconvenient Truth Behind Waiting for Superman,* received a standing ovation at a Friday night screening.

I was surprised to learn that a few days earlier, the march organizers had rebuffed an offer to meet with high-level White House officials. "July 30th is your opportunity to listen to us," they wrote in a public statement. "After the march, we will be open to meeting with White House or Department of Education leaders to further discuss our specific proposals." When we gathered on the Ellipse on

Saturday, I was proud to be among educators who decided that their arguments would be more effectively delivered in the streets than in the Oval Office.

Among the speakers was actor Matt Damon, whose speech was galvanizing: "From the time I went to kindergarten through my senior year in high school, I went to public schools. I wouldn't trade that education and experience for anything." Damon wasted no time getting right to the point—the obsession with testing and "data" is killing real education:

> I had incredible teachers. As I look at my life today, the things I value most about myself—my imagination, my love of acting, my passion for writing, my love of learning, my curiosity—all come from how I was parented and taught. And none of these qualities that I've just mentioned—none of these qualities that I prize so deeply, that have brought me so much joy, that brought me so much professional success—none of these qualities that make me who I am . . . can be tested.

As an elementary school teacher, I understand the impulse that educators often feel to shrug off these big political questions, to just close their doors and "make the best of it." It was thoroughly inspiring to march with educators and activists who aren't just fighting *against* corporate reform and privatization, but are fighting *for* progressive education. I wish more of my coworkers could have been there.

The Save Our Schools march wasn't perfect. I would like to have seen some of the teachers I met at the conference speaking from the stage on Saturday. Clearly, there needs to be a more conscious effort to bring the younger echelons of our ranks on board and a special outreach to parents of color. But overall, I was impressed with what the organizers were able to pull off with so few resources. For their vision and hard work, they deserve our praise and sincere thanks.

For their political courage in declining the White House's invitation, they deserve our support and solidarity.

The SOS march laid down a historic marker. I left Washington feeling that perhaps we are finally on our way to building a truly independent, nationwide movement of parents, teachers, and students in this country that can fight for the kind of high-quality public education system we desperately need.

Kim Dominguez, born in Tucson, is a Chicana feminist, Mexican American, and Raza Studies alumna, as well as a student and organizer. Bob Peterson, currently president of the Milwaukee Teachers' Education Association, is a thirty-year elementary school teacher in the Milwaukee Public Schools and a founder of Rethinking Schools *and La Escuela Fratney. Stephanie Walters is an organizing consultant for the Wisconsin Education Association Council and an editor of* Rethinking Schools. *Kathy M. Xiong is a National Board–certified teacher currently teaching special education in the Milwaukee Public Schools district. Sarah Knopp has been a teacher and union activist in the Los Angeles Unified School District since 2000. Gillian Russom teaches at Roosevelt High School and is East Area chair of United Teachers Los Angeles. Brian Jones is a teacher, actor, and activist in New York City.*

25.   Another World Is Possible/ Another Education Is Necessary

Bill Ayers

Hope is a choice; confidence is a politics. We don't minimize the horror, but neither are we stuck in the thrall of it. Hope is an antidote to cynicism and despair; it is the capacity to notice or invent alternatives, and then to do something, to get busy in projects of repair. Because the future is unknown, optimism is simply dreaming, pessimism merely a dreary turn of mind. Hopefulness, on the other hand, holds out the possibility of change. We choose to see life as infused with the capacity to cherish happiness, to respect evidence and argument and reason, to uphold integrity, and to imagine a world more loving, more peaceful, and more just than the one we were given. Of course we live in dark times, and some of us inhabit even darker places, and, yes, we act mostly in the dark. But we are never freer as teachers and students, citizens, residents, activists, and thinkers than when we refuse to see the situation or the world before us as the absolute end of the matter. Whatever *is* the case stands side by side with what *could* be or *should* be the case. Choose life; choose possibility; choose action.

Schools As They Are

While many teachers and students long for schooling as something transcendent and powerful, we find ourselves too often locked in institutions that reduce learning to a mindless and irrelevant routine of drill and skill, and teaching to a kind of glorified clerking, passing along a curriculum of received wisdom and predigested (and often false) bits of information. This is unlovely in practice, and it is unworthy of our deepest dreams, for a community that excludes even one of its members is no community at all.

The dominant metaphor in education today posits schools as

businesses, teachers as workers, students as products and commodities, and it leads rather simply to thinking that school closings and privatizing the public space are natural events, relentless standardized test-and-punish regimes sensible, zero tolerance a reasonable proxy for justice—this is what the true believers call "reform."

Schools for obedience and conformity are characterized by passivity and fatalism and infused with anti-intellectualism and irrelevance. They turn on the little technologies for control and normalization—the elaborate schemes for managing the crowd; the knotted system of rules and discipline; the exhaustive machinery of schedules and clocks; the laborious programs of sorting the crowd into winners and losers through testing and punishing, grading, assessing, and judging, all of it adding up to a familiar cave, an intricately constructed hierarchy—everyone in a designated place and a place for everyone.

Education As It Might Be

If we hope to contribute to rescuing education from the tangle of its discontents, we must rearticulate and reignite—and try to live out in our daily lives—the basic proposition that all human beings are of incalculable value, and that life in a just and democratic society is geared toward and powered by a profoundly radical idea: the fullest development of all human beings—regardless of race or ethnicity, origin or background, ability or disability—is the necessary condition for the full development of each person; and, conversely, the fullest development of each is necessary for the full development of all.

In a democracy, how can we justify one school for wealthy white kids funded to the tune of $40,000 per student per year, and another school for poor immigrant kids or the descendants of formerly enslaved people with access to $4,000 per student per year? How do we excuse an overcrowded one-hundred-year old school building that looks like a medieval prison with a rotting roof and a busted furnace down the road from a generously appointed campus containing well-maintained athletic fields and an Olympic-sized pool as well as a state-of-the-art physics lab in a building that looks like a palace for learning? That reality offends the very idea that each person is equal in value and regard, and reflects instead the reactionary idea that some of us are more deserving and more valuable than others.

The rearticulation of the ideal that each human being is of infinite value, the one and only who will ever trod the earth, has huge implications for curriculum and teaching as well, for what is taught and how. It points in the first place to the importance of opposing the hidden curriculum of obedience and conformity in favor of foregrounding and teaching initiative, questioning, doubt, skepticism, courage, imagination, entrepreneurship, and creativity—these are central and not peripheral to an adequate twenty-first-century education. These are the qualities we must find ways to model and nourish, encourage and defend in our communities and our classrooms.

Good schools are not monastic cells, nor isolated and separate spaces. Classrooms are necessarily porous places, connected to families and communities, and they ought to be even more so. After all, every student represents dozens, scores, countless others whose hopes and experiences are riding alongside. Imagine any classroom, any space with or without walls, where people assemble with an expectation of teaching and learning. Teaching in the twenty-first century and in a humane society based on principles of equality, justice, and basic human rights must have some special defining feature— even if only theoretically or speculatively or aspirationally. What makes a classroom powered by a vision of freedom and enlightenment unmistakable?

In a just and free society, teachers want students to be able to think for themselves and develop minds of their own, to make judgments based on evidence and argument, and to build capacities for exploration and invention. Youth tend to ask the most fundamental and essential questions that are, like the young themselves, always in motion, dynamic, and never twice the same: Who in the world am I? How did I get here and where am I going? What in the world are my choices and my chances? What did I learn that the teacher didn't know? What's my story, and how is it like or unlike the stories of others? What is my responsibility to those others? In many ways, these kinds of questions are themselves the answers, the very frame of a forward-looking curriculum; keeping these questions vital, alive, and fresh is a huge challenge as we search for ways to live within and beyond the contingent and partial answers, as well as the setbacks, discovered and encountered along the way.

Educators who are today oriented toward justice and liberation and enlightenment as living forces and powerful aspirations focus their efforts not on the production of things, but on the production of fully developed human beings who are capable of controlling and transforming their own lives, citizens and residents who can participate actively in public life, people who can open their eyes and awaken themselves and others as they think and act ethically in a complex and ever-changing world. This kind of teaching encourages students to develop initiative and imagination, the capacity to name and constantly interrogate the world, the wisdom to identify the obstacles to their full humanity and to the humanity of others, and the courage to act upon whatever the known demands. Education, then, is transformed from rote boredom and endlessly alienating routines into something that is eye-popping and mind-blowing—always opening doors and opening minds as students forge their own pathways into a wider world.

Children and their families are the central and natural concern of teachers, and a commitment to their humanity is a sensible starting point. Any honest and moral accounting of the lives of students sweeps immediately into the wider world, to the grinding effects of poverty, the widening gap between the haves and the have-nots both here and around the globe, the horrors of war, and the gaping abyss of environmental catastrophe. We cannot pretend to be child- or youth-centered and at the same time ignore the concentric circles of context that both shape young people's lives here and now, and illuminate the possibilities and perils they will face in the future.

All children need to develop a sense of the unique capacity of human beings to shape and create reality in concert with conscious purposes and plans. This means that our schools—both within and way beyond the existing institutional spaces called "school"—need to be transformed to provide children ongoing opportunities to exercise their resourcefulness, to solve the real problems of their communities. Like all human beings, children and young people need to be of use; they cannot productively be treated as "objects" to be taught "subjects." Their cognitive juices will begin to flow if and when their hearts, heads, and hands are engaged in improving their daily lives and their surroundings.

Just imagine how much safer and livelier and more peaceful our neighborhoods and communities would become if we reorganized education in a fundamental way; instead of trying to keep children isolated in classrooms, envision engaging them in community-building activities with the same audacity and vision with which the Black Freedom Movement engaged them in desegregation work forty-five years ago: planting community gardens, recycling waste, creating alternative transportation and work sites, naming and protesting injustices around them, organizing neighborhood arts and health festivals, broadcasting a radio show, researching the local waste system, rehabbing houses, painting public murals. By giving children and young people a reason to learn beyond the individualistic goal of getting a job and making more money, by encouraging them to exercise their minds and their hearts and their soul power, we would tap into the deep well of human values that gives life a richer shape and meaning.

Instead of trying to bully young people to remain in classrooms isolated from the community and structured only to prepare them for a distant and quickly disappearing and hostile job market, we might recognize that the reason so many young people drop out of schools is because they are voting with their feet against an educational system that sorts, tracks, tests, and rejects or certifies them like products in a factory. They are crying out for an experience that values them as human beings. With our eyes open, we cannot now easily or even sensibly accede to a regime of test and punish, certainly not the widely discredited institutional fraud known as the No Child Left Behind initiative, nor the rebranded but essentially identical

Race to the Top program. We need to reimagine education as a basic human right focusing on the full development of human potential, on justice, joy, and peace.

The new millennium and new conditions challenge us to start imagining an entirely new world with new approaches to production and consumption and participation, as well as wildly new relationships with one another and wholly new educational possibilities. It suggests the need for schools of equity and engagement driven by and serving the needs of the rising majority and of all humanity. It insists that we notice, construct, or revive models of liberatory education, reject and resist the top-down, irrelevant, straitjacket schools we have, and strike out for alternatives: participatory democracy at every level and in new and innovative ways; problem-posing, question-asking, and humanizing curricula; student- and community- and family-led schools; classrooms without walls conducted in the streets and parks and workplaces and playgrounds—all of these ache to be invented and initiated, not in Washington policy parlors but on the ground, from the bottom, in the communities.

In schools as they could be, education would be constructed as a fundamental human right geared toward the fullest development of the human personality, and the reconstruction of society around basic principles of equality and justice and recognition.

Nine Possible Steps, Campaigns, and Connections

1. This is our city, this is our education. Imagine the creation of vast, messy, democratic community assemblies that are organized explicitly to draw on the wisdom of everyone to rethink and renew curriculum and teaching, and the meaning and location of school.

2. The "Septima Clark Teacher Corps." Imagine a massive initiative to bring parents and unemployed folks into the schools as aids and teacher candidates, and to bring school people into communities as peers and colleagues.

3. Peer restorative justice. Imagine building in every school and every community a movement to end the criminalization of youth, and to open creative spaces for moral reflection and positive action,

redemption and recovery, whenever someone has made a mistake or wronged the community.

4. Take the profit out of education. Imagine a giant upheaval to put an end to privatizing the public space.

5. Rethink and redesign assessment. Imagine groups of parents, teachers, and students fighting to end valorizing test scores as a proxy for intelligence, worth, or achievement, and moving away from high-stakes, sort-and-punish approaches, toward authentic assessment.

6. Toward equity and simple justice. Imagine a popular drive to end to segregation based on race, class, ability, status, or background in terms of access and funding.

7. Demilitarize our schools. Imagine drawing a bright line between military training and recruitment, and education as a human right.

8. No excuses. Imagine a community focus on reclaiming "accountability" and "standards" as they apply to every institution and entity, not teachers alone or students in isolation. After all, high asthma rates, health disparities, poverty, access to guns, militarization, consumerism as an ideology (and more) cannot sensibly be laid at the feet of teachers; they are the responsibility of all, especially the wealthy and the powerful.

9. Connect the dots, reframe the debates. Each of these possible campaigns and initiatives has the potential to unleash enormous popular power to reimagine, reframe, and rebuild education from the bottom up. Whatever we initiate, whatever we take up and organize around, let's remember to connect the dots, see the links, and unite the issues.

Bill Ayers, formerly Distinguished Professor of Education and Senior University Scholar at the University of Illinois at Chicago, writes about social justice, democracy and education, and teaching as an essentially intellectual, ethical, and political enterprise.

Postscript

The stories in this book as well as in For Further Reading represent countless acts of courage and hope taken nationally and globally to resist the ambush of public education. As time goes on, attacks on public education will have taken new forms, and new approaches to resistance will have emerged. While initiatives will change, the stories in this book embody the individual commitment, collective action, and courage that we will need as we move into the future.

More recently, the Occupy Wall Street movement galvanized millions of people to think in new ways, as well as to "occupy" locations of power and privilege across the nation and the world. Educators, students, teacher unions, and parents have actively embraced the idea that "We are the 99%." Through this new lens, we better understand how the 1 percent—corporate and education CEOs, venture philanthropists, and top-level government officials—have hijacked public education for profit at the expense of the 99 percent. We recognize that as the 99 percent, we are both *served by* public education and *dependent on* it to maintain our democracy. Even in the face of opposition, the power of the 99 percent can be formidable if we speak up and act together.

The contrast between the public will and public policy is stark in public education, as it is in all areas of our lives. Most teachers, parents, and students, for example, clearly think that the high-stakes testing mania hurts education, yet the top-down policies that depend on testing continue to be imposed. It is time for the public will to drive public policy.

Amy and David Goodman write, "Protesting is an act of love. It is born of a deeply held conviction that the world can be a better, kinder place. Saying no to injustice is the ultimate declaration of hope."[1] The authors of *Educational Courage* model various means of protest aimed at taking back public education for the public good.

1. Write, Speak, and Spread the Word

Write about your experiences of the ambush of public education and share your analysis and critique. Write letters to the editors, speak at school board meetings, write a blog, or—like the Kids As Self Advocates—publish your work. Tell your story from the heart and challenge the sound bites in the mainstream media with authentic, personal stories.

2. Educate Yourself by Accessing Alternative Media Sources

There is much to learn and the information is readily available. The corporate media will not tell you about the many others resisting the ambush of public education today—and there are so many! Seek out voices of critique and action.

Subscribe to *Rethinking Schools,* visit the FairTest website, and join their Listservs. Listen to *Democracy Now!* to better understand how the attempt to privatize public education is part of interlocking initiatives to privatize health care, housing, and virtually all other parts of our lives. Feel the energy of knowing that you are part of a broad, powerful movement. Use the resources and organizations on the *Educational Courage* website to help you connect with others.

3. Harness Your Courage and Say No

Saying no to injustice takes courage. And it sends a powerful message to others and creates new possibilities and power. Even when no means resigning from a job, it can lead to opportunities more consonant with your values, as Neha Singhal found when she quit Teach For America and enrolled in a master's program in social justice education. When declaring "I won't be part of this," look for allies. When Latricia Wilson challenged the Tennessee high school exit exams, she found others willing to support her, developing a community of resistance.

4. Use the Cracks

Don't just say no; also say yes! As you go about your daily work, look for the cracks and widen them. As educators, you can raise students' and parents' critical consciousness about the unfairness of high-stakes testing at the same time you work to help students pass them. Raise critical awareness about the connections between what's happening to public education and other neoliberal initiatives, as Jessica Klonsky did by teaching about the Iraq war. Help others see the bigger picture and critique, for example, how dysfunctional our national funding priorities are; decreases in funds for education are integrally tied to increased spending on war.

5. Organize and "Occupy"

Reach beyond your immediate workplace to organize with others. As educators, you can look for allies in your school and form a group to take on policies that hurt both students and educators, as Katie Hogan did. Look to the practices of social justice unionism, as Bob Peterson, Sarah Knopp, and Gillian Russom did, to push your union in a more progressive direction and to build coalitions with many other groups working for equity in your community.

Join a social justice educator group in your area and, if there is none, form one. The collective voices of parents can also be powerful. Learn from the strategies of Juanita Doyan, Julie Woestehoff, and the other parent writers and apply them close to home.

Join broader actions when you can. Don Perl's Coalition for Better Education couldn't travel to the Save Our Schools march in Washington, DC, so it held its own rally on the same day in Colorado. Connect with movements that challenge the neoliberal policies that affect our lives, both nationally and globally. Educators, parents, and students marched in Occupy actions and created their own initiatives, such as Occupy the Department of Education in New York City, where they occupied a board meeting. They protested the expensive imposition of Common Core Standards and more testing onto schools that were in disrepair and that had just faced significant increases in class size. Build coalitions of parents, educators, students, and taxpayers who together are the 99 percent.

6. Maintain Vision and Hope

Public education *can* be different. We can remember, contrary to the corporate agenda, that public schools can be spaces of cooperation, caring, altruism, and concern for the common good. By finding and honoring these very examples in our schools today, they can be magnified manyfold as we work together to resist the ambush of public education. And we can find strength for the long haul in Miles Horton's wisdom: democracy is a long-term project.

Historian and activist Howard Zinn offers us inspiration to that end:

> To be hopeful in bad times is not just foolishly romantic. It is based on the fact that human history is a history not only of cruelty, but also of compassion, sacrifice, courage, kindness.
>
> What we choose to emphasize in this complex history will determine our lives. If we see only the worst, it destroys our capacity to do something. If we remember those times and places—and there are so many—when people have behaved magnificently, this gives us the energy to act, and at least the possibility of sending this spinning top of a world in a different direction.
>
> And if we do act, in however small a way, we don't have to wait for some grand utopian future. The future is an infinite succession of presents, and to live now as we think human beings should live, in defiance of all that is bad around us, is itself a marvelous victory.[2]

The way *you* act every day—with courage and hope to resist the ambush of public education and work for just, democratic public schools—is itself a marvelous victory.

—Nancy Schniedewind and Mara Sapon-Shevin
December 2011

Notes

1. Amy Goodman and David Goodman, *Standing Up to the Madness: Ordinary Heroes in Extraordinary Times* (New York: Hyperion Press, 2008), 216.

2. Howard Zinn, *You Can't Be Neutral on a Moving Train* (Boston: Beacon Press, 1994), 208.

For Further Reading

The following essays may be found on the *Educational Courage* website, www.beacon.org/educationalcourage.

These additional narratives of courage and resilience, coordinated with the book's sections, offer powerful stories from others who have resisted the ambush of public education.

Acknowledgments

We acknowledge the outstanding, ongoing work of the writers whose pieces appear in this book and on the *Educational Courage* website for their powerful stories of resistance and hope.

Their many contributions to the fight for more democratic schools are inspiring. We also deeply appreciate all those whose stories couldn't be shared here but who inspire us with their persistence and tenacity in the face of injustice.

Readers at Rethinking Schools and Stan Karp, in particular, provided valuable feedback. North Dakota Study Group folks provided ideas and inspiration. We value Lisa Edstrom's fine ideas and hard work on preliminary book material. We are thankful for the skill and perseverance of Philipa Meyers, Kelly Collins, Ryan Solomon, Yosung Song, Michelle Mondo, Betty Marton, and Lisa Petro, who have contributed to collecting, editing, and preparing these accounts for publication.

Nancy thanks David Porter, Dan and Jesse Schniedewind, and Mara thanks Karen and Peppy Sayers, and Dalia and Leora Sapon-Shevin for their ongoing help, encouragement, and support.

Educational Courage: Resisting the Ambush of Public Education is truly a collective endeavor that reflects the commitment of many across the nation who speak out and act to create more democratic schools and a more democratic society.